LOVE
LEADERSHIP

LOVE
LEADERSHIP

What the World Needs Now

Gregg Cochlan

New Voices Press

NVP

Published by New Voices Press
www.newvoicespress.com
Phone: 212-580-8833
Fax: 212-501-9582
info@newvoicespress.com

First publication: January 2008

An application to register this book for cataloguing has been
submitted to the Library of Congress.

ISBN: 0-974813-6-3
1. Business 2. Motivational 3. Inspirational 4. Self-help

Love Leadership™ is a registered trademark of Gregg Cochlan

Cover design by Gordon McKay, Studio A Design

Book design by BYJ Communications

Website design by Keith Feldenstein

Printed in the United States of America

For more information:
www.loveleadership.com

"I tell college students, when you get to be my age you will be successful if the people who you hope to have love you, do love you...I know people who have buildings named after them, receive great honors, etc., and nobody loves them – not even the people who give them honors...

Wouldn't it be great if we could buy love for $1 million? But the only way to be loved is to be lovable. You always get back more than you give away... There's nobody I know who commands the love of others who doesn't feel like a success. And I can't imagine people who aren't loved feel very successful."

~Warren Buffett

TABLE OF CONTENTS

Acknowledgements

Introduction by Lou Tice • *11*

Preface • *13*

1. What Love Leadership Is, and Why We Need It • *21*

2. Journey to a "New Normal" • *35*

3. The Importance of Principles to Love Leadership • *51*

4. Discovering the Value of Authenticity and Vulnerability • *61*

5. Courage: The Gateway to Fearlessness and Adventure • *69*

6. Good Beyond Self: The Deepest Meaning of Love • *81*

7. The Importance of Love Followership • *93*

8. Overcoming Conflict the Love Leadership Way • *103*

9. The Evolution of a Love Leader: Progress not Perfection • *113*

10. Can Love Leadership Resonate Globally? • *121*

Afterword • *129*

A Conversation With Gregg • *135*

Suggested Reading • *141*

About the Author • *147*

Acknowledgements

Writing this book has been profound learning experience. One of the biggest contributors in terms of learning, not just to this book but to my life, is Lou Tice. For more than fifteen years, Lou has taught me, through The Pacific Institute, his books and his personal coaching, to look at human behaviour in a whole new way. I consider myself most fortunate to be associated with Lou and owe him a profound dept of gratitude.

There are also a number of business leaders who may not have known what a great influence they have had on me by their actions. Just a few are Gord Farmer, Jim Hutch, Tom Laird. Dennis Lyster, Fred Townley-McKay, Karen Anderson, Ron Enns, Lana Doke, and many others. The leader I refer to often throughout the book is Myrna Bentley, CEO of Concentra Financial, with whom I had the good fortune to work over a 10-year period. During this period she emerged as the very model of an effective Love Leader. I am forever indebted to Myrna.

My colleagues at The Pacific Institute need to be recognised for their modelling of how love can be part of your business and, in fact, increase your performance. I also received such wonderful support from many of my friends at TPI, especially Christy Watson, Barbie Seifert, Laura Knutson, Dr. Glenn Terrell, Ron Medved and Jack Fitterer.

From the very beginning of this project, I knew I was woefully lacking in my ability to turn my thoughts into well-written words. This project would never have gotten off the ground without the faithful support and mentorship of Bev Fast. Bev, thank you for being there at the very beginning.

To my book project team, Bonnie Egan, Gordon McKay, Shannon Brunner, Bruce Jacobson and Keith Feldenstein: guys, your research, edits, design and creativity made this project a wonderful experience. Thank you. To my brilliant and demanding book collaborator, Judy Katz, all I can say is "I love you."

To my friends—thank you so much for your constant encouragement and the truthful sounding boards you provided.

Specifically I need to thank Dave Derksen, who acted as my coach and Love Leadership guide, always ensuring I was true to myself and true to the integrity of intent of the book.

I have been so fortunate to have been surrounded my whole life with a family—my parents, sisters, aunts and uncles, who gave me love unconditionally. My family made giving love just a normal part of life.

Lastly, I want to thank my wife Sandra, who has always supported me unquestioningly, no matter what I choose to do. This project was no different. Through our 28 years of marriage, Sandra has always made me a better person because of our loving partnership. To our children, Brogen and Avery, I have learned so much from you. You have enabled me to understand what love is just by the way you so freely give love to me. You challenge me to continue to progress. To my eldest daughter Katie, the same holds true for you. But I also need to let you know how much I love the way you allow me to be authentic and show my vulnerability. Your love strengthens me.

And to you the reader, I love you too, simply for picking up this book and giving me the chance to share all that I have learned. I hope I have sufficiently challenged you to have the courage to act on it. That kind of courage is what the world needs now.

Introduction

A Simple, Profound Solution for Our Time

Until this book, I don't think I've ever seen the words "love" and "leadership" linked together, especially when it comes to the corporate world. There are dozens of books out there on every aspect of leadership, but to put "love" and "leadership" together takes a balance of heart, brains and courage—qualities I have come to expect from Gregg Cochlan.

I met Gregg about ten years ago when he came to Seattle to see if the work of The Pacific Institute matched up with his own purpose in life. Immediately, I could see the tremendous potential in this quiet Canadian. Even then, Gregg was a man of the head *and* heart. Fortunately for the Institute, Gregg could see the synergy. Since then, Gregg has worked with countless organizations across Canada and here in the United States. It is that work experience, and his own keen eye for people, that has produced Love Leadership.

Diane, my wife, and I, began The Pacific Institute nearly 40 years ago, with the express purpose of making change—the word that strikes fear into the hearts of even the strongest of individuals—easy and stress-free. Each of us has the capacity within us to create our own lives, tapping into the potential that lies dormant within. In fact, I believe it is the responsibility of each of us to become all that we can be. And when we do, we become leaders of our own lives, and examples to others.

To be a leader doesn't require a formal title. In fact, I find that the informal leaders within any organization have more power, if you will, than any title can give them. Why? Because they have earned the respect of those with whom they work. It's not about leading with charisma or the current cult of personality. These individuals, while they may be charismatic, have shown that they do not take lightly the trust and respect they have been given.

I used the word "courage" earlier, and I did it on purpose. Some folks will probably snicker at "Love Leadership" since we tend to have so few definitions for the word "love," at least in North America. We have become as afraid of the word as we have of the emotion. Perhaps it is because the word has been overworked, and the entertainment media only shows us one facet of the emotion.

If you look up the definition of the word "love" in Webster's Unabridged Dictionary, you will find nearly 30 different definitions. One in particular refers to love as "affectionate concern for the well-being of others." That pretty much sums up Love Leadership—leading with concern for the well-being of others on your teams and in your work groups, and likewise for your family and communities. Indeed, it is, or should be, a term that resonates with affectionate concern for the well-being of the world and its future.

How different would the world be today if humans had embraced leadership from the aspect of love rather than competition, and of being in community for the benefit of the whole rather than needing to be "over and above"? That world, I believe, is one we would all want to live in. Fortunately for us, there is still time. Fortunately for us, Gregg has the courage to show us how.

After reading Gregg's book, which I believe every one of us should, worldwide, the question then becomes simply this: As leaders, do we have the courage to make this ideal he so vividly describes into a reality?

I hope so. Because I wholeheartedly agree that Love Leadership is what the world needs now. It is these sets of principles that guide and inform the work of The Pacific Institute here and in all the dark corners of the world. As a leader I know that I have made a commitment to myself to evolve past my old football coaching style of command-and-control and allow love into my leadership in everything I do. For everyone who wants to likewise evolve, this book will spell out exactly what is needed, and what you, as one individual, can do, to spread the love, and the light, in your own corner of the world.

My advice is to trust the process. Again quoting Gregg, "It's no longer a good to have, it's a got to have." The rewards will be beyond your wildest dreams.

LouTice

The Pacific Institute, Seattle, WA
July 31, 2007

Preface

Simply put, this book is about allowing love into your leadership. It is also about increasing your capacity to love, not just your family but also the people you work with, your community and your world. Further, it is about maturing to a point in your evolution where you can generate an infinitely higher level of respect for the dignity and humanity of all individuals. In this book I am going to show you what can happen to you, to your business, and to the world when you increase your capacity to love, and no longer compartmentalize it, so that love permeates every area of your life.

The Buddha said, "The thought manifests as the word. The word manifests as the deed. The deed develops into habit. And the habit hardens into character. So watch the thought and its ways with care. And let it spring from love, born out of concern for all beings."

To me, the concept of Love Leadership is the all-important next step on the world stage, and it is not merely a "good to have" but a critical "got to have." Nor is it a feel-good rehash of a New Age philosophy. Instead, as I will show you in the chapters ahead, it is, or should be and *must* become, a highly effective, serious, ultramodern, results-driven brand of leadership—one that, as I hope you will agree by the time you finish reading this book, is urgently needed in this the lightning-speed communicating, rapidly shrinking, 24/7 networked, human global society in which we now live. Because, like it or not, this is a world from which there is no turning back.

Think about the word itself. LOVE. That one word has unique power like no other. We all tend to use the word lightly, and thus trivialize it, as in "I love chocolate." Yet, being told "I love you" by someone we care about is a personal validation that can actually change the very molecules in our bodies. One researcher who proved this is Dr. Masaru Emoto, author of the best-selling *The Hidden Messages in Water* (Beyond Words Publishing, 2004). In his experiments, Dr. Emoto wrote the word "love" on paper and positioned the paper with the word on it near water. He then studied the crystalline formations. Next he changed the written word to "hate." The changes in the structure of water were immediate and dramatic. Somehow "feeling" the word love (I don't pretend to fully understand this, but his results have been verified) the water itself made beautiful patterns, while proximity to the word "hate" (and a few other negative words he used) caused the water to assume tight, defensive, essentially ugly patterns.

As Dr. Emoto concluded, "There is an intrinsic vibrational pattern at the atomic level in all matter, which is the smallest unit of energy. Its basis is the energy of human consciousness, and words alone can have a profound effect." This concept of a vibrational pattern is called "hado," and has been accepted in Japan for thousands of years.

If this sounds far-out to you, think about it in terms of your own experience—and not just when you hear the words "I love you" from a beloved's lips. Think about the difference that small loving *gestures* make: a warm hug, a touch, a smile, a kind word, a listening ear, an honest compliment, or the smallest act of consideration. Think about the transformational power of love, and again, *not the word alone*, but the love of others, rather than the domination of others. Think about how resilient, courageous, adventuresome and *full* you are when you feel loved. Think about the intrinsic happiness you feel when you give love. In many cases, it doesn't even need to be said, just felt. This book is about how allowing love into your leadership can make you perform better, and how it will do the same for the people you lead.

To be completely clear, this book is not about the word but rather the *action* of love. What I have found is that to move or influence people, you must enter their intellect through emotion. Although knowledge is indeed power, to change behavior, feelings are more effective than facts, and affecting people's feelings engenders a deeper, more memorable experiential process than simply imparting information.

Imagine what could happen if (and, hopefully, when) that becomes a dominant principle in the culture of U.S. and Canadian corporations, and corporations around the world. And also, again hopefully, when a Love Leadership style begins to permeate the halls of academia, hospitals, non-for-profit organizations, the military...in fact, all arenas of human endeavor and all areas where human beings interact. Can you envision how the effects might resonate throughout the country and the planet, like the ripples that flow in ever-widening circles? Or like a song being sung by one person and then another and another until that song resonates around the globe. Imagine how deep and broad this could get! The possibility sends shivers down my spine.

The uniqueness of Love Leadership

What differentiates Love Leadership from other styles of leadership—for example, the classic, top-down, Newtonian "command-and-control" style, which I will discuss later on—is that a Love Leader is one who treats those under, beside or even above him or herself with respect, fully appreciating and regularly acknowledging their contributions toward the greater good. The qualities inherent in a Love Leadership culture, which is based more on a Whiteheadian model, as I will also explain in more detail, are flexibility, co-responsibility, compassion, and *respect for the unconditional protection of the dignity of the individual.* Love Leaders: of the individual are authentic, principled, courageous, open, inclusive, humanistic, accountable, and able to admit mistakes and show vulnerability. The freedom of Love Leadership inspires creativity and adventurousness. This culture will also attract abundance—that is, love draws to it more love and more rewards. Simply put, the more you give the more you get.

Using the word "love" to express how you feel about the people you work with is not always well-received in a business setting. That being said, what I have discovered in the course of my career—a discovery that continues to astonish me daily, and is the foundation, the bedrock if you will, of my work as a leadership coach—is that, when those who lead others are willing to bring that basic human emotion into their roles, absolute miracles occur. People thrive, businesses prosper, customers are happy, and the vibrational pattern is a positive one for the world at large.

Love Leaders: Love Leaders are not perfect human beings. They are, however, willing to do things in a way that is not always easy. They are willing, for example, to allow people their dignity, even when they have to provide negative feedback on job performance, fire an individual, or painfully "excess" large numbers of people when cutbacks can't be avoided. Love Leaders also have the courage—and make no mistake, it can take courage—to appropriately express their deep affection for the people they lead, whether or not they use the actual word love, as we shall see in some of the true examples ahead.

Where my work truly began

The genesis of Love Leadership as my personal calling stems from four episodes, beginning over ten years ago, in which I personally experienced the awesome power of the word love, and, more importantly, the power of love in action.

The first episode took place early in my career. I had spent several years managing people in a corporation of some 4,500 employees, where one of the teams I led had, over time, developed an amazing synergy that allowed us to consistently produce extraordinary results. One day, at a meeting with another group within the same company, someone verbally subjected a fellow on our team, although he was not present, to a barrage of unwarranted criticism. I objected, and concluded my defense with "I love Dave."

While the people around the table did not say anything, eyes rolled and looks of amusement were exchanged, as if some embarrassing secret had just been revealed. Perplexed by that cynical reaction, I began to ask myself how we had gotten to this point in corporations, where a simple statement like that was suspect, even taboo. It was very much an "aha moment" that a phrase I considered normal would be met with such a critical response. Perhaps this should not have surprised me as much as it did, given the corporate conditioning on what is considered normal and abnormal to which we have traditionally been subjected. No matter what factors were at play, it was upsetting to me that my having expressed my feelings in that way was seen as abnormal.

While I was mulling this over, still working at that large company, I became associated with The Pacific Institute (TPI), based in Seattle, where I sought to further invest my personal and our teams' leadership development through the TPI curriculum.

The pioneering work of The Pacific Institute

The Pacific Institute is an international corporation, founded in 1971 by Lou and Diane Tice. Its mission is to provide educational curricula based on the foundations of modern cognitive psychology and social learning theory. Their intention is to empower individuals by allowing them to recognize and access their ability to choose growth, freedom and personal excellence. One of my most powerful lessons was in learning how thinking affects performance and that I (like everyone else) always act in accordance with the truth as I believe it to be, even though my truth—or yours—may not necessarily be the "real truth," if there even is such a thing. The danger, I learned, is that, for example, if I formed a truth that "love is not part of leadership," I might base my actions on that belief rather than on what was intuitively true for me—in this case, that love is a part of leadership.

In 1997, I left my employment and began a full-time consulting practice of my own, which I call "*Thinc,* Corporate Change Architect," affiliated with The Pacific Institute. During this period, I attended a three-day community-building workshop on team development that was also attended by several men and women who were my new colleagues at TPI, where we would all be freelance leadership coaches. The workshop was based on the philosophy of Dr. M. Scott Peck, an inspirational speaker who wrote the bestseller, *The Road Less Traveled.* This was the longest, most in-depth involvement I'd had with my new colleagues at TPI, and it allowed us the opportunity to see who each of us was and what we were all about.

At this point in my life I was becoming much more comfortable saying what I felt and speaking authentically. I was now prepared to be vulnerable and even a little courageous. I knew that in being authentic and fully self-expressed, I could potentially be judged negatively by the group. I was willing to risk it, so I did express myself fully with those people on those days.

A natural connection, revealed

On the final day, one of the leaders of our team, a woman named Sheri Atteridge (who has since become a valued friend), passed me a note. What she wrote was, "You are so authentic with our team. People are attracted to your loving leadership." Reading her words, which made me feel both valued and validated, I suddenly saw myself differently. I saw clearly not only who I was but also what I was trying to do to help others. Those few simple words had a profound effect on my life. I began to see the strong, natural connection between leadership and love. More importantly, I realized that I *was* a loving leader and that it was not just okay to be one; It appeared to me to be far more effective than any other style of leadership.

A few years later I got a call for my services as a leadership consultant. The caller, Myrna Bentley, had been promoted from within to the position of CEO of a major financial services company in Canada. Myrna, having been with the company for many years, had been conditioned to operate in the common "top down" management style, and had consequently cloaked her authentic self in order to fit in and succeed in the corporate culture. However, Myrna also knew there was a different style, one that would be far more authentic for her. Like many executives who rise to the top of their organizations, Myrna had uncomfortably adapted herself to fit an authoritarian management style. She also knew this was not really who she was, and that this style would not work in the new culture she wanted to create in her company. In essence, she felt trapped in a false persona.

After being led successfully out of near bankruptcy by the previous CEO, the company had reached a plateau. Despite its many successes, the company was struggling to get to the next level. While the past CEO had used command-and-control techniques, which were appropriate and effective for the immediate crisis, a new corporate culture was clearly needed.

Myrna was completely open to working with me to find a better way to work collaboratively with her top executives as well as with the entire company. Newly confident in my ideas about Love Leadership, although I had not yet begun to call it by that name, I asked Myrna, "Is there a different approach we can take to leadership?" Delighted to be "real" and now given permission through my coaching to lead in a style that came so naturally to her, she created a culture of Love Leadership that allowed her to propel the company to become the flourishing $4 billion corporation it is today. In fact, the company prospered so dramatically that it was rated number one in "best practices in business and industry" by the Conference Board of Canada, as well as earning accolades elsewhere as one of the "50 Best Managed" and "100 Best Places To Work in Canada."

Telling people you work with that you love them, publicly

I clearly recall with great emotion and pride the day that Myrna was invited to speak at the annual conference of The Pacific Institute. This event is a prestigious symposium that is attended by 800 or more business leaders from all over the world. Myrna's presentation was greeted with a rousing ovation. After the applause died down, Myrna walked to the front of the stage, individually named every person on her staff in the audience, and told them each publicly that she loved them.

The next day, another speaker, the head of a South African company, began his address, and stood for a moment in thoughtful silence, quivering slightly. The next thing he said was, "I have learned here that it's okay to tell people I love them, and I will." He then said "I love you," by name, to every single member of *his* team who was present. The audience sat mesmerized, clearly moved by the courage of this big man to break from the norm and speak from his heart.

As I listened, it occurred to me that a lot had happened since the time I defended a colleague by blurting out "I love Dave." Now here I was, listening to people say "I love you" publicly to their colleagues, male and female alike. And it was not only okay with the hundreds of people in attendance; it was being celebrated and applauded as a best business practice!

Increasing the capacity to love

Sitting in that auditorium, I recalled a word association game I used to play with my kids that involved connecting two incongruent words. Like explorers seeking new territories, we'd try to think of two words that had never been put together before, like "scuba and salad" or "briefcases and bananas." Now love and leadership, two words that might have seemed equally odd together, no longer seemed incongruent. In truth, they were like the two magnets I sometimes roll around in my pocket. Once in a while, the magnet halves would accidentally come together so forcefully that they stuck, and formed a combined unit. The combination of these two words, the concept they created, now made perfect sense. And this was apparently true, not only for me, but also for a growing number of others.

Recently I had another epiphany. I realized that the quest I am on (and perhaps I sound like a Don Quixote, but I'm willing to risk it) is to increase my own capacity to love, and to love not just my immediate family but the entire human family, the community we are all a part of, whether we know it or not. Recognizing this, I can only hope that, by using whatever powers of persuasion I have, I can stimulate your capacity to love others, and convince you to use your newfound abilities on a leadership level and in all aspects of your life. That is what I try to do, daily, in mine, for no other reason than this: we need it. It is what the world needs now.

> *"To work in the world lovingly means that we are defining what we will be for, rather than reacting to what we are against."*
> ~Christina Baldwin

Chapter One

What Love Leadership Is, and Why We Need It

While my studies in the field of leadership were deliberate and purposeful, I had never studied the field of love. Like most people, I just lived it the best way I could. When the two came together in my mind, forming the new concept I call Love Leadership, it seemed purely accidental. Then again, there are those who say there are no accidents. In any case, I've studied that combination, love and leadership, for some time now, and I can tell you with absolute conviction, based on observation and experience, that when leadership is accomplished with love, it is simply infinitely better than if done any other way.

After college, I still didn't know what I wanted to do with my life. One of the first companies I worked for was SaskTel, the local telephone company. There I started out as a lineman, a physical job that involved mostly outdoor work. Fortunately, SaskTel was a progressive company heavily invested in its people, and they'd give you as much training as you were willing to take on, with lots of opportunity for advancement. Most people, I noticed, seemed to be either too hesitant or perhaps not sufficiently ambitious, to hold their hands up and volunteer beyond their assigned duties. But I was always hungry. Even after a long day on the job, I'd say "I'll do that!" Over the next 17 years, I moved from union to management, and eventually worked my way into senior management.

My education in leadership actually began when I became an Internal Performance Consultant at SaskTel. In that capacity, I worked with a vice president and 75 or 80 managers in either executive or management positions. Through this job I became interested in all aspects of human behavior. The thing that intrigued me most was that I could look at the different skills and successes of these various managers and see what worked and what didn't. As I coached them, I was also observing and learning from them—a most interesting two-way street.

Good leaders both get and give respect

One of the things I noticed first was that the most consistent traits in the good managers/ leaders/ bosses/ foremen/ supervisors were that they were honest, forthright and straightforward. If there was an employee issue, they didn't dodge it, but instead dealt with it with respect. They demanded respect, of course, but they also *gave* respect. That was the first quality, I learned, that makes a person a great leader.

The next thing I learned was the importance of really getting to know who you are and what you stand for. I was in my early 30s and I didn't have a good sense of what I stood for. Yet here I was meeting these 40, 50 and 60-year-old managers, and my job was to help them do *their* jobs better. "Well, Gregg," I told myself, "you'd better figure out what you stand for." I began to read everything I could put my hands on about leadership, including Stephen Covey's best seller, *The Seven Habits of Highly Effective People*. I learned from Covey's speeches and his book that another key ingredient of good leadership—and it's a critical component, no matter what kind of leader you are—is to be principle-centered, the "true north" of leadership. Armed with this understanding, I began to encourage each would-be leader I coached to develop his or her own set of principles.

To me, each of us is innately as much of an expert on leadership as Stephen Covey or other noted leadership gurus. You've got to internalize whatever works for you. However, what I was also learning is that there were certain key traits that seem to be essential to good leadership, and principle-centered leadership is definitely one of those.

Another key trait is authenticity. The people I admired most were very authentic. I soon saw that becoming authentic is part of the maturation process, because it's impossible to be authentic when you don't know who you are. When you're a young person trying to figure out "Am I this?" or "Am I that?" you are, in essence, trying on identities to see what fits. As soon as you do get a strong sense of your true identity, you can begin to enrich it by creating more depth to that persona. That's where character and principles begin to meld. You get the authenticity going, you add principles, and then you strive to become increasingly consistent in following your principles. With that in place, you begin to develop your essential character.

Principles and authenticity make decision making easier

Interestingly, the more authentic you are, and the more principled you are, the easier it becomes to make the right decisions. People who have difficulty making decisions are those who don't know themselves. People who know what they stand for and have strong convictions can make good decisions. They are more effective leaders because there is no pretense in them. I should note here that the definition of a good decision is subjective. There are leaders who are authentic and clearly stand up for what they believe in, but some may not be principled. Hitler, Idi Amin and other dictators come to mind.

Like many authors and teachers on leadership, I could go on and on and list the "Ten Traits of Good Leadership," most of which you will have heard before. Instead, I want to suggest the one characteristic that is rarely connected to leadership, and that—as you will have guessed—is love. Discovering this "secret" paralleled my personal growth as I began to better understand the meaning of love, primarily through my growing family. At the same time, I was beginning to understand that leaders who were the most effective did allow love into their leadership, albeit at times cleverly disguised. After all, we all knew it was, and in many cases still is, socially unacceptable to show love at work.

As my strength as a leader grew, what was also emerging was my *ability* to love, and to show that love. This, incidentally, is not a pose. It's authentically who I am. Over time, I decided that I'm not going to hide that aspect of myself, because, for me, hiding it would not be authentic.

I have discovered that as soon as you start to behave in a loving way, more often than not, you begin to see people responding back in a loving way. I also saw that, from a business perspective, when people act lovingly, fear is driven out, and when that happens, performance improves exponentially.

Putting a name to the concept

An interesting thing happened with the last team I managed at my old company, where we truly loved each other even though we didn't openly say so. Today we all still see each other, and the first thing we do when we get together is hug each other—whether male or female. Back then, I was trying to see if we could create that kind of loving culture in the company, and we did. It was just my natural tendency. Finally, as far back as 1997, I put a name to this leadership style I had been developing—and called it Love Leadership. Since then I have been working on myself to consistently act with love and also to encourage others I work with or coach to discover the power of love. It's been over ten years now that I have continued to practice, think about and refine this new leadership style.

Even so, when I set out to write this book, I at first felt compelled to come up with a different word. I had come from 20 years of corporate conditioning that says you don't EVER use the "L-word" in business—that love has no place in the business world. To find a different word, I looked in the dictionary and scoured the thesaurus. There had to be some other word I could use—but there wasn't! So here I am, despite my conditioning, using the "L-word" in a book on effective leadership—and telling you that Love Leadership in today's environment is not only viable, but also that it can be more effective and more productive than any other style.

Using all the tools in the toolbox

I'm not suggesting that Love Leadership is the only style, but I am saying that this attitude, this brand of leadership, overlays other tools, other approaches. There are times when every leader needs to take a command-and-control approach. But what happens if that approach becomes your dominant style? Command-and-control says "I know the way. Follow me...*or else.*" It seeks to align everyone else to the senior leader, with deviation neither expected nor tolerated. Command-and-control might sometimes work well when the dominant force is in the room, but is not so good when he or she leaves. The goal of leadership is to get people to perform at a high level whether you are there or not. At the opposite end of the scale are leaders who strive for an empowering, participatory style, but that can only be achieved if it is aligned with a common focus.

There is an old matrix that shows different approaches leaders can take. As the graph below illustrates, on the X axis is Alignment, and on the Y axis is Empowerment. The challenge for a leader is

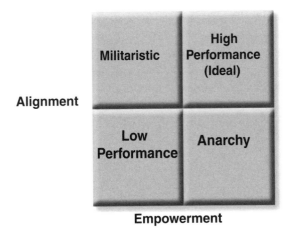

how to get the right degree of both alignment and empowerment.

Demanding alignment can result in a militaristic style of leadership. Swing too far to total empowerment, and you may find yourself in anarchy.

The secret is to not get trapped in one approach and make that your style. If you do, you'll block yourself and minimize your effectiveness. In other words, there are times we need alignment and times we need empowerment. However, to just *demand* alignment will not get it for us. And if we just encourage empowerment we may not get alignment. A Love Leader encourages both and provides opportunities for people to get to the upper quadrant on the graph, a balance between alignment and empowerment, which is the ideal.

The Love Leader has an overarching style. If you don't have that to anchor your approach, you will lose focus and clarity. If there's no constancy or authenticity to who you are, people will misread you or misinterpret your actions. You will also feel unsettled and frustrated. Events will seem outside your control, and people won't respond the way you want or expect them to. These are symptoms of poor leadership. Love Leadership works to balance these two approaches. You as a leader provide clarity in your direction but respect the capability of your people to figure out the "how." And yes, it always comes back to *you!*

Attributes that make up Love Leadership

Such attributes as authenticity, vulnerability (the ability to admit mistakes or show weaknesses), principle-centeredness, courage, fearlessness, good beyond self, abundance and mentorship are all part of a Love Leadership style. Most important is the willingness to love. The basic foundation of all of these is a respect for other people. You must always uphold the human dignity of each person and of people in general. And, by nurturing these attributes in yourself, you come closer to your core as a Love Leader. The interesting thing about Love Leadership is that you not only get love back, you get these valuable additions: co-responsibility, co-accountability, adventurousness, and teamwork at its best.

The myriad benefits of Love Leadership

Love Leadership frees you. It lets you do more than you thought you could. The consequences of unleashing that kind of love in corporate relationships and business settings is that neither you nor your people are afraid to try something new, and by so doing, possibly make mistakes.

Reflect for a moment. Think about the times in your life where you felt loved, or even better, when a group of people—family, friends, co-workers or teammates—felt loved. It's a thrilling experience that raises you to another level, transports you to a higher plane. When you inject leadership into that love, you are infused with spirit that inspires your people to rise to yet another plateau. Your ambition and confidence grow and your ability to act authentically and without fear increases. That step between feeling confident and sparking higher performance requires you to be authentic and courageous enough to show vulnerability, all from a philosophy of "good beyond yourself." Taken together, this adds up to creating a fearless culture. The end result, in my experience, is higher performance and greater results.

Incidentally, my advising you to show vulnerability is not to suggest ignoring self-preservation. We did not, as a species, evolve over millions of years by doing so. One should always look both left and right when crossing the street. My mother taught me that when I was five years old.

Because Love Leadership is authentic, it gives you permission to be who you are. It is fearless—and it does take courage to tell your co-workers, "Hey, I don't know all the answers. What do *you* think? How can *we* make this work?" Love Leadership creates a culture where work becomes a great adventure. It prepares you and your team to take risks, and allows all of you to better adapt to change.

I was once working with a group of CEOs and asked them this question, hoping it would get them to dig deeper, "What do you know for sure?" After a few minutes of reflection, they jointly came to the conclusion that there are two things they knew for sure:

1) Change is constant, and
2) Resistance to change is equally constant.

After coming to those two conclusions they thought some more, and decided that there was a third thing they knew for sure: that as leaders they couldn't really control the speed or complexity of change but that, also as leaders, they *could* affect the way their people responded to change. Based on the fact that fear is the greatest contributor to creative avoidance behavior, they concluded that *they need to drive fear out of their organizations.*

Love Leadership helps you affect the ability of your staff, your executives, and your board to accept rather than resist change. Through your leadership style, you can create a more adventure-some group that not only adapts to change—they welcome it.

It's all about results

Love Leadership is not a hug-fest. I say that somewhat defensively because in using the L-word I wonder if it becomes easier for you, as readers, to write off this leadership style as something "nice" or "feel good," but not practical. The truth is, Love Leadership is not about being nice or feeling good—it's about getting results.

Those who practice Love Leadership do not do it because they want people to like them, although that in itself is fine. Good leaders are people who unleash the talents, the energy, the innovation and the creativity of the people and teams in their companies or organizations. The bottom line is that they want to maximize organizational performance. Their experiences and personal philosophies have shown them that the best way to do this isn't through threats but with love. There are quantifiable results to a Love Leadership style, and that's the whole point of leadership—results.

What Love Leadership is and is not

Many business books today focus on the practical management side of leadership—best practices, challenges and responses, what works, what doesn't, and why. This is all good stuff. However, my focus is, I believe, significantly different. My intent here is to explore the actual nature of leadership and in so doing lead you to a better understanding of the power of this new paradigm.

I'll be the first to say that to succeed as a Love Leader you absolutely need a knowledgeable foundation in good management. With any innovative idea, there can be a huge chasm between the idea and how it can be implemented. Therefore, yes, you must have an understanding of what it means to manage effectively. That said, let's look at what Love Leadership is and what it is not.

There's a simple exercise I often employ when I'm facilitating strategic management or board planning sessions, because I believe it helps people focus closely on the essence of a thing— what it is, what it is not. I've already enumerated some leadership attributes that are key qualities. For example, in Love Leadership, showing vulnerability is a strength; in command-and-control, it's a weakness. Why? Because in Love Leadership, showing vulnerability unleashes your authenticity. It's okay to make a mistake because you're not a "title," you're a human being, and being human means you can't always be right.

Love is nonjudgmental and forgiving

One of the beautiful aspects of Love Leadership is that it allows you to observe rather than judge, and opens the door to learning for everyone, including *you!* I believe this new "level" of leadership is a natural evolution that would fit into many organizations.

Love Leadership means:	Love Leadership does not mean:
• You care about people first;	• You don't care about profit;
• You look for the good first;	• You don't see the bad;
• You have clear faith in people; and	• People don't let you down; or
• You are prepared to show your feelings.	• You hold hands with or and hug everyone.

Love Leadership as an evolution in business

Love Leadership itself is not new. The "Love Leaders" of yesteryear include Mahatma Gandhi, Mother Teresa and Martin Luther King. It's difficult to compete with saints and martyrs, nor would I ask that of you or of myself. However, despite some evidence to the contrary, I do believe we as a species are moving toward a higher consciousness, one more respectful of human diversity and dignity. As I write this, the conflicts in Iraq, Afghanistan, the Middle East, Africa and other countries might seem to stand in sharp contradiction to this statement. But, stepping back and looking at global evolution from 1,000 years ago to 500 to 100 years ago, straight through to the present, can put things in a different perspective. We can see a continuum in which our compassion for others has grown, and our tolerance for violence, poverty and racism has diminished. To see the bigger picture, you need to change your viewpoint. It's like pushing up the visor on your car and suddenly realizing how much more you can see of the road ahead.

A shift in our collective consciousness

What I see ahead is more than the evolution of management theories and practices. I see an evolution of people, of our social culture. I see people maturing to a new level and not being as willing as before to support automatic "knee-jerk" reactions. For many, their view on war, for example, seems to be moving from seeing it as a "normal" event to considering war as abnormal. I personally find it tremendously *immature* when leaders cannot resolve conflicts without fighting. If there's a conflict between your kids, do you just let them hit each other, or do you call a "time out" and have them start talking? When the Bush Administration announced it was going to invade Iraq, there were demonstrations all over the globe—people expressing opposition. That opposition continues to increase. I see that as a positive. I'm not a historian, but I see an evolution toward a more peaceful world—which includes our evolution into a leadership style that compels people, individually and collectively, to work out peaceful ways to resolve conflicts on every level of human commerce.

Love Leadership is not about gender

One big hurdle to Love Leadership that I have observed is when people hold to the belief that Love Leadership is a feminine style. There are now many men who are strong Love Leaders. No doubt, there is more acceptance of showing or expressing love among females than among males. Still, I believe this is changing. For me, Love Leadership has no gender. It's about how we approach our relationships with other people and the common and individual environments we create. As a society we need to ask ourselves why love is considered an exclusively feminine characteristic. Aren't we *all* capable of love? Perhaps the problem lies in what we perceive as feminine and masculine traits and accepting that it's our conditioning that assigns a gender value to them.

Love Leadership is not about drawing on male or female attributes; rather, it's about staying true to who you are as an individual, regardless of gender. At the 2004 TPI Global Conference, where Myrna Bentley made such an impact by publicly declaring her love for her staff, several people came up to her and asked, "What's your secret to success as a woman leader?" Myrna replied, "Continuing to be a woman." She packed almost twenty-five years of experience into that short sentence, and she wasn't advocating a feminine versus masculine style of leadership. She was simply saying, "Be yourself."

Why it's tough to "just be yourself"

As I have repeatedly observed, many of those who move successfully up the ranks in business have chosen to adapt their natural leadership style to an already established style within the organization. This is especially true for women. On the one hand, society is more accepting of women who demonstrate loving, nurturing behavior; conversely, it also richly rewards women business leaders who move away from emotional or "feminine" styles to more "masculine" leadership styles.

Assertiveness versus aggressiveness is a good case in point. Women in leadership roles are often called aggressive when they

LOVE LEADERSHIP IS	LOVE LEADERSHIP IS NOT
❑ Abundant	❑ Cold
❑ Accountable	❑ Closed
❑ Adventurous	❑ Commanding
❑ Authentic	❑ Controlling
❑ Compassionate	❑ Ego-Based
❑ Courageous	❑ Guarded
❑ Good Beyond Self	❑ Judgmental
❑ Humanistic	❑ Sexual Attraction
❑ Inclusive	❑ Withholding
❑ Open	❑ Protective
❑ Principle-Centered	❑ Ambivalent
❑ Vulnerable	❑ Wishy Washy
❑ Results-Driven	❑ A Hug Fest

are being assertive. They are admiringly said to "act like men." But this kind of statement should offend male and female leaders equally. I do not believe being a man automatically means I have to be aggressive, nor do I believe an assertive female leader is displaying masculine traits. This next statement may offend women, but I think some women leaders, in their attempt to be assertive, overdo it and become overly aggressive. This may also be true of men, but for some reason it is more acceptable in men. In my observation, aggressiveness doesn't work for either gender—it inspires an aggressive or passive response in those being led, neither of which leads to effective performance.

In their book *Competing for the Future* (Harvard Business School Press, 1994), the authors, management consultants Gary Hamel and C.K. Prahalad, assert that winning in business today is not about being number one. It's about who "gets to the future first." To that end, they urge companies to create their own futures, envision new markets, and reinvent themselves. They call the tendency of people in power to reward behavior and characteristics that are similar to, or the same as, their own "corporate genetic cloning." We all tend to surround ourselves with people who see things similarly and believe in the same things as we do. In other words, like attracts like. However, as the authors maintain, and I agree, this limits your options, because, by simply following the norm, you cannot look at things in a different way. And what if the norm is wrong?

Setting a corporate culture in concrete

I often use the metaphor of "poured concrete" to describe established corporate cultures. When you pour concrete, you fit it into a pre-set form that has already been framed out. The wet concrete flows only where you want it to, and then hardens in place. Corporate culture *is* like concrete. Over years and years of old-style leadership, certain characteristics set a framework for leadership and patterns of behavior become established. But businesses change, world events change, and often that permanent, "hardened in place" culture may no longer serve you well. Like concrete, the only way to change it is to get a jack-hammer to break it apart. Lou Tice calls this culture "an intense invisible force that is there to perpetuate itself." That's why it's so tough to be yourself in some corporate cultures—the mold is set.

If you're a leader looking for a different way, after you read this book, I hope that the different way will be through Love

Leadership. If it is, be prepared to pull out the jack-hammer, because you most likely *will* have to bust up the "concrete" before serious change can begin. It may be difficult, but it is going to be well worth the trouble…as you will soon see.

> "When we are motivated by goals that have deep meaning, by dreams that need completion, by pure love that needs expressing, then we truly live life."
>
> ~Greg Anderson

Chapter Two

Journey to a "New Normal"

The meaning of "normal" is subjective. What's normal for you may be abnormal for me and vice versa. It is interesting to consider how what's normal for you, or for me, becomes "the norm" in our lives. We humans can make almost anything seem normal. Love Leadership is my normal, and to me it should be the universal "new normal." Here's one illustrative and moving story of what some tolerate as normal.

A couple of years ago, one of my colleagues at The Pacific Institute was working with a group of young people who were caught up in the ongoing gang violence in Los Angeles. At one point, they took a break, and this colleague went for a walk with a participant, a 15-year-old girl. When the teenager paused to look at a red dress in a store window, my colleague thought she heard the girl say, "I'm going to get married in a red dress." Puzzled, she asked, "You mean girls don't want to get married in a white dress anymore?" The girl looked at her with surprise and said, "I didn't say 'married.' I said 'buried'." As my colleague stood there stunned, the girl went on to tell her, ever so matter-of-factly, everything she had imagined for her funeral—who would be there, who would serve as pallbearers, what songs would be sung, what eulogy she wanted them to say, and what her friends would be doing. In her world, funerals of youths like herself were taking place every day. For her, this kind of outcome to her young life was normal. For most of us, this tragic mindset is *not* normal. Nor should it ever be accepted as such, for to do so is resignation.

The above figure is used by The Pacific Institute to help describe how thought turns into reality. The top circle is the conscious mind where we perceive "reality." We associate our conscious perceptions with our stored truths, decide what we believe, and then act accordingly. At bottom left is the subconscious mind, where beliefs and truths are stored. The bottom right-hand circle is the creative subconscious mind. As human beings, we store "truth" in the subconscious mind, but what we store as true may not actually be "true" in any absolute sense. The "job function" of the creative subconscious mind is to maintain sanity—our sense of what's normal. Our creative subconscious works overtime to maintain what we define as normal stored in our subconscious. Now the question becomes: what *is* normal? The 15-year-old girl in our example had stored the truth that, given her environment, her life expectancy was short. This kind of belief system can affect us individually and organizationally. It can also happen collectively to a community and to an entire nation.

I am proud to say The Pacific Institute is involved in many projects, past and present, designed to help create a "new normal." On a global basis, TPI has initiated conversations about what's normal and what is not. Two places where TPI has worked to establish a "new normal" are Northern Ireland and Guatemala. Currently, there is a peace in Northern Ireland, and of course this can change overnight. Now I know the history is far more complicated, but for the past 200 years, it was normal for a Catholic to hate a Protestant and a Protestant to hate a Catholic—a seemingly intractable conflict. From the outside, we wondered why the two sides—both Christians—could go on killing each other. When that state of conflict is stored in the subconscious mind, people act in accordance. If and when they get to peace, it doesn't "feel" normal. We can now only hope and pray that sanity will be restored and that peace will eventually become the new normal in Northern Ireland.

In Guatemala, the situation is similar. Guatemala had 35 years of civil unrest, which became the norm. Children grew up in that kind of unsettled and unsettling environment. When peace was restored, people didn't know what to do with it. The volatile situation calmed down but people still felt they needed conflict to maintain their sanity. What was normal for them is absolutely abnormal for almost everyone else, and in that nation that kind of discomfort still lingers. Hopefully, there will eventually be a "new normal" without the kind of conflict Guatemalans have lived with for two generations.

Newtonian	Whiteheadian
Is-ness: meaning it is the way it is	Flexibility
Predictability: the organization is very predictable	Co-responsible
Stability: Everything needs to be steady	Co-accountable
Fearful	Fearless
Power is hierarchical	Power is spread out horizontally
Ideas are linear and rational, and can at the extreme be pragmatic and rigid.	Ideas are nonlinear, multidirectional; they collaboratively and creatively build and feed off each other.

The evolution of two sharply different leadership styles

Two distinct leadership styles have traditionally dominated Western society and influenced policy and decision making in every institution, from countries and corporations to organized religions. The first can be broadly categorized as *Newtonian* and the second as *Whiteheadian,* after Isaac Newton and Alfred Lord Whitehead.

Isaac Newton's worldview was, essentially, that God created a perfect world and man messed it up. In order to return to the perfection God created from the chaos that humanity created, and will continue to create when left to its own devices, leaders need to put rules and regulations in place. The result is a rigid, power-oriented, hierarchical leadership style. In this kind of organization, employees take orders from the senior executives and the hierarchal style is carried from the top down. This can only work if there is a high degree of adherence to principles in the leadership. As we have seen in companies like Enron, this style can result in leaders who plunder their companies for their own gain and, to cite just one tragic result, leave long-term, loyal employees without their pensions. Even if the leadership is honest, Newtonian leaders will never be able to get the highest performance out of their workforces, simply because such leaders cannot inspire their workforces to care enough about the company.

The other worldview, the Whiteheadian, is radically different. Alfred North Whitehead, a mathematician and philosopher, proposed that while God created the universe, that universe is constantly evolving, and mankind's role is to contribute to this evolution. In today's business culture, the traits of this leadership style include flexibility of roles, along with co-accountability and co-responsibility. While the Newtonian style is a pyramid, with the leader at the apex, the Whiteheadian model is more like a sphere, surrounded by other spheres. In this approach, whoever has the most knowledge, experience or skill is, or should be, the one who leads.

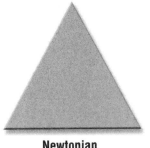

Newtonian

Whiteheadian

W. L. Gore & Associates (Gore-Tex, Glide dental floss), is an example of a Whiteheadian organization. CEO Terri L. Kelly explains the corporate culture:

> *The idea of me as CEO managing the company is a misperception. My goal is to provide the overall direction. I spend a lot of time making sure we have the right people in the right roles. You know the joke, "I'm from corporate, and I'm here to help." We don't need un-useful, un-valuable corporate help. We empower divisions and push out responsibility. We're so diversified that it's impossible for a CEO to have that depth of knowledge—and not even practical.*
>
> *How we work sets us apart. We encourage hands-on innovation, involving those closest to a project in decision making. Teams organize around opportunities and leaders emerge.*
>
> *Our founder, Bill Gore, created a flat lattice organization. There are no chains of command, nor predetermined channels of communication. Instead, we communicate directly with each other and are accountable to fellow members of our multi-disciplined teams...*
>
> *Associates (not employees) are hired for general work areas. With the guidance of their sponsors (not bosses) and a growing understanding of opportunities and team objectives, associates commit to projects that match their skills. All of this takes place in an environment that combines freedom with cooperation and autonomy with synergy.*
>
> *Everyone can quickly earn the credibility to define and drive projects. Sponsors help associates chart a course in the organization that will offer personal fulfillment while maximizing their contribution to the enterprise.*

Leaders may be appointed, but are defined by "followership." More often, leaders emerge naturally by demonstrating special knowledge, skill, or experience that advances a business objective.

The Whiteheadian style is the one that provides the platform on which Love Leadership is built. It recognizes that the human condition is not static but changing, and that as the human race evolves, leadership styles will evolve with them.

Love Leadership as the "new normal" for family and friends

Happily, there is a slow but steady movement toward Love Leadership. For one thing, there are more visible demonstrations of love by men. It begins in the family. Go to any school event, playground or park and watch parents interact with their kids. Thirty years ago the chance of seeing a dad openly showing affection to his daughter may have been possible, but certainly you would rarely see affection publicly show to his son. Fast forward to the present. You'll most likely see fathers hugging their sons as well as their daughters, and participating in family activities as much as the mothers are. These days, there is more connection between parents and kids overall. It is also now more socially acceptable to love and care for other people. That's a generational change—and the start of a "new normal."

For generations people have been afraid of the word "love," except in certain narrow contexts. I can tell you that my dad, like many of his generation, was extremely frugal, if not completely restrictive, when it came to either saying or displaying love. It seems like many fathers were like that, and my dad was no exception. He was afraid to use the word "love" almost all of his life. The feeling was there, the caring was there, but, for him, a punch on the shoulder was, and still is, a more acceptable way of communicating it. Interestingly, as he ages this has changed for the better. Not long ago he dropped my 18-year-old daughter, Katelyn, off at the airport. She was going through the doors when he called her back. "What do you want, Papa?" she asked. He said, "I just wanted to tell you that I love you, Kate." Katelyn did a double take. Her "papa" had never said "I love you" to her before. But at 78 years old, he seemed to be thinking the way I did when, already an adult, I said it to *him* the first time. He doesn't want to take the chance that he will leave it unsaid.

I use my dad as an example because I believe he's representative of his generation. For him, the whole idea of an emotional expression of love, even with his family, let alone the people he worked with, just wasn't acceptable. It wasn't normal. This restrictive behavior spilled over into the workplace. So if it wasn't appropriate at home, by gosh, it sure wasn't appropriate at work. Today, thankfully, it is much more acceptable to my generation, and especially to younger people.

Men saying "I love you" more often

From a male perspective, we're seeing this evolutionary progression in the family. As a young person, it was not normal for me to tell my friends that I loved them. As I mature, it's more normal for me to do that. Now I hear my kids unselfconsciously telling their friends that they love them. I need to put this next story in context even though I did share this with my son before I used it. He was fine with my telling of this story. Nevertheless, like a hangover from yesteryear, a boy telling another friend that he loves him does run some risk.

My 14-year-old son, Brogen, loves many of his friends and they love him. They don't need to say this, but on occasion sometimes it slips out. I happened to overhear a conversation Brogen had with his friend, Brady. Just before he hung up the phone, Brogen said, "I love you, too." Obviously, Brady had just said "I love you" to Brogen. These are 14-year-old boys! So this appears to have become a new normal for their generation. The conclusion I have come to is that my capacity to love is greater than my dad's and I'll bet that my son's capacity for love will be even greater than mine. The evolution, or perhaps *revolution*, is on!

Another favorite story of mine is about my daughter, Avery. When Avery was about ten years old, a friend named Tarah was having a difficult day. She was over at our house and she was upset and crying. Avery asked if she wanted a glass of water and Tarah said yes. Avery took a little bit of time to get it, but when she brought the water, she was holding the glass in a certain way to hide something about the glass and, as she turned it toward Tarah, Tarah stopped crying and hugged Avery. Avery had taped a piece of paper on the glass that said, "We love you Tarah." I could see right there that my daughter already had a tremendous capacity for love. As a child, this is normal and instinctive; as we grow up somehow our culture and our social norms make what should be normal feel like it is abnormal. That is the challenge we all face.

Love is everywhere

A father expressing his love for his son in public has reached the realm of sports. Under head coach John Thompson III, Georgetown had their first victory over a No. 1 team in more than 20 years. As reported in *Georgetown Magazine* (December 14, 2006), after the game, the coach navigated through the roaring crowds to find his legendary father, former Georgetown head coach John Thompson Jr. "Congratulations, I love you," the father said to his son as he embraced him. A few months later, Patrick Ewing was in Georgetown to watch *his* son, Patrick Ewing, Jr., play for Thompson's team. The *Los Angeles Times* (April 1, 2007) reporter asked the younger Ewing what his famous dad said after the game. "Just that he was proud of me and he loved me," Ewing said. "A lot of people don't get to hear that from their parents."

More love expressed in the macho world of sports

While it is completely common and acceptable for people to express their affection for a favorite team using the word "love," as in "I love the Yankees" or "I love the NFL," hearing a guy say he loves another guy who is not a relative (or an admired athlete) has always been viewed with suspicion. Imagine my surprise when I heard the word as I watched the NBA playoffs. Larry Brown was coaching the Detroit Pistons. It was the last timeout of a pivotal game. After the timeout, the players headed back to the court. Suddenly Brown called them back for a huddle. Everyone in the audience was wondering what last minute message he'd given them, especially since right after that the team went on to win the game.

During the post-game wrap-up, a reporter asked one of the players what strategy or inspirational tactic Brown had for them at that moment. He said, "Oh Coach called us back and said 'Guys, I just want to let you know I love you.'" Wow. No tactics, no trickery—just the real thing. And I'll bet there wasn't any eye-rolling when he said it.

Brown, by the way, is clearly comfortable with the L-word. In a recent TV interview about his possibly coaching the Charlotte Bobcats in the next season, Brown responded. "As far as Charlotte goes, everyone knows I have a very special relationship with Michael (Jordan). I've known him for years. So saying 'no' to him would be almost impossible for me, just because it would be hard for me to say 'no' to him about anything. We're family, and I love him." Some people may remember that Larry Brown has not always acted so lovingly toward his players. Sure, he's human, like everybody else. I'm just saying that here's another man able to express love in leadership. And I'm guessing Brown isn't the only guy who feels comfortable saying he loves his team or teammates. It's odd because in the most masculine arena, sports, it is more normal now to do that than it's ever been. I think it means we're moving to a new normal.

Prioritizing family time: another new normal

Today it's okay for a man to show his love for his family. Actually, I would argue that it is a man or woman's natural instinct, but that we have been conditioned *not* to show it, *not* to say it. Now we're showing and saying it—making it the new normal. As soon as this shift happened within the family, it had to move to the workplace, and bring the emotions that come with family into the workplace. It's a natural step. That's what Love Leadership does: it moves all the elements of personal growth we seek to attain in our personal lives over into our work lives. Today, for example, younger people aren't as willing to work 70 to 80-hour workweeks because they have family priorities. This all helps provide a better balance between work and family. If you think about employees in the context of their families, the shift toward Love Leadership in the workplace is…normal.

How does this new normal fit into Love Leadership? For the most part, love in corporate leadership has been seen as abnormal. Years and years of corporate conditioning has made it unacceptable to even imply love between coworkers or leaders and staff in a corporation. However, what I am seeing is that the protective gear is being removed, piece by piece.

Changing the "acceptable" leadership in business

The 1980s was an era that saw a lot of downsizing. Many companies needed to downsize in order to survive. That often meant letting go of large numbers of people. Sadly, in many cases the way it was done was about as unlike Love Leadership as you can get. It was common to hear or read newspaper accounts of mass firings and the "hatchet" men who made this experience unnecessarily brutal. In my city, a well-known local company had been bought by a national chain, and the changeover led to the termination of 100 people. Rumors about the sale and its impact had run rampant through the organization for months, leading up to the company's sale. Morale was as low as it could get.

When the sale finally went through, the parent company sent in an agency to do their dirty work. They marched 200 of their employees into a meeting at a local hotel—on a Saturday no less. As they entered the hotel, each person was given an envelope. If you got envelope A, you went into one meeting room and learned that your job was safe; if you got envelope B you went into another room to hear someone say "You're fired." The bad feelings engendered throughout the organization and city by this brutal and unnecessary process still rankles today, years later. At the time, many people considered this "normal" corporate behavior. In actual fact, this was a leadership choice, and a bad one at that.

Downsizing or firing people with dignity and respect

Apply Love Leadership to the same situation. The company would still have had to cut 100 jobs, and that still would mean telling 100 people "Sorry, you're all out of work." But when you're driven by compassion, the way you do the deed is entirely different. Love Leadership never forgets the dignity of the individual. You may have to fire people, but you don't have to degrade them. You bring a high level of humanity to carrying out the task.

These people could have been told individually rather than in a "herd" that they would have to be let go. It could have been done gently and kindly. The company could have shared their full rationale for the dismissal so each person would know that their dismissal was not personal. They could have been provided with outplacement services and counseling. These are just a few examples of how Love Leadership can show up under even the toughest, most challenging situations. The people who were summarily fired could and should have been prepared for the change in advance—in fact, as soon as the leadership found out that downsizing would be necessary. I will talk more later on about strategies and methods, and how Love Leaders can handle specific situations. But I hope I have made the *need* for a new normal abundantly clear.

A natural Love Leader on a journey to the new normal

Myrna Bentley, the President and CEO of Concentra Financial, a long-time client and a good friend, is one of the truest Love Leaders I have ever known. However, back in 1997, when I first began working with her, this quality was not at all evident. Myrna had had twenty years of conditioning that taught her to mask her natural style in order to fit a more Newtonian corporate culture. As we came to know each other, I witnessed many moments where Myrna revealed her natural leadership style—and I saw that her authentic way of being, when she allowed it to show through, was profoundly effective. Eventually, together, we set out to normalize another style of leadership that would go beyond the standard top-down, command-and-control approach and tactics she was used to using.

Myrna is an excellent model of how the real world application of a Love Leadership style can literally turn a corporation around. The corporate culture Myrna grew up in was highly perfectionistic. This permeated the organization. Everyone, from the executive office down to the rank and file, was fearful of making a mistake. If you did, you felt it. It was an environment that inspired risk avoidance and fear of change. That turned out to be a big problem. In the 1990s the financial industry, just like most other industries, was undergoing revolutionary changes. It wasn't business as usual anymore, and yet that's where Myrna's organization, Concentra, was stuck. About 10 or 15 years previously, Concentra had found itself in an organizational crisis. The CEO was a traditional command-and-control personality, and he *was* able to steer the company back to fiscal health. However, his leadership style didn't work well in the change-driven environment of the 1990s. What was so brilliantly successful in helping the organization survive and regain financially stability did not work in helping it grow.

Myrna steps into her Love Leadership style

The retirement of the CEO signaled a changing of the guard. Myrna stepped forward as the leading candidate and was appointed CEO by the board. From the beginning, she took a different approach, one that involved teamwork, compassion and supportiveness. Within a year of assuming the position, she had won the respect and support of the board. The question that might be developing for you is how did she do this? Simply stated, Myrna exhibited all the attributes of a Love Leader. Over the next several chapters I will clarify these attributes that she and her executive team put into action.

Today that company is financially successful and consistently held up as an example of a great place to work. Myrna doesn't claim this success as a personal achievement. "We did it together as an organization," she says, adding that "Love Leadership is an excellent leadership style, but it's not an individual achievement. You need others to buy into it to create an environment or culture that is based on Love Leadership."

Saying "I love you" at Southwest Airlines

Herbert D. "Herb" Kelleher is the co-founder, Chairman and former CEO of Southwest Airlines. In an article he wrote for "Leader to Leader" (Thought Leaders Forum, 1997) Kelleher reveals himself to be a Love Leader:

> *Our real accomplishment is to have inspired our people to buy into a concept, to share a feeling and an attitude, to identify with the company – and then to execute. Because our low-fare strategy is so central to who we are, our employees are enormously cost-conscious. We don't have the traditional budget struggles at the end of the year. That's not to say that we don't argue over budget allocations, but it's rare that a manager submits an inflated budget thinking, "If I ask for 200 percent more, maybe I'll get 100 percent." That's just not us.*
>
> *But you need to spend more time on the intangibles than the tangibles to create that kind of buy-in. For example, I have told our people in the field – mostly young people – that my hope is that when they're talking to their grandchildren, they say that Southwest Airlines was one of the finest experiences they ever had; that it helped them grow beyond anything they thought possible.* **We are not afraid to talk to our people with emotion. We're not afraid to tell them, "We love you." Because we do.** [emphasis added]

The challenge in making love the new normal

Unbecoming conduct can always be rationalized by claiming that "everybody does it." If everybody in a corporation shows the same disrespect, that can, unfortunately, become fixed in place as normal. Many companies do show disdain and disrespect for a division, a department, a leader, a group, or an individual. This is a bad practice that will unquestionably come back to haunt you. My argument—and, in fact, the basic message of this book—is that we can and must create a new normal that will filter this out, and that we can do so by allowing love into our leadership.

When I was 20 years old, I liked my friends, I cared about them, but I wouldn't have said I love them. As I mature, I find I now have a much greater capacity to love my friends. The depth of my relationships progresses through family to friends, to teams, to companies, to communities, to countries—and to caring deeply for the whole planet. As you progress in life, your capacity to have deeper relationships evolves. What the world needs now, quite frankly, is to increase our capacity for caring about people other than ourselves. If you look at the individual progression we go through, our ability to care for and love people increases as we get older. Collectively, I believe, the human race is maturing, and our capacity to care and love people in a broader spectrum is increasing.

Love for one another is a natural energy, from birth to death. When babies are born, we love them. When people are dying, there's nothing more important to them than to feel they are and have been loved. On a personal level, we hold both of those expressions of love, for the young and for the old, to be precious. Yet on a corporate level, we don't show that same respect and caring for the individual. For me, that's *abnormal.*

Chapter Three

The Importance of Principles to Love Leadership

My grandpa was a man who strongly believed in such old-fashioned principles as honesty and integrity. I still carry the money clip he gave me. I've had it so long now that I don't think twice when I pull it out, but every so often I again become conscious of its true meaning. Not long ago, I went to an office supply store to buy a printer cartridge. I found the cartridge I wanted and brought it up to the counter. The sales clerk convinced me to buy the two-pack as the better bargain. Somehow I left the store having paid for the two-pack cartridge, but with all *three* cartridges in my bag—and the detector had not gone off. When I got to my car and looked in the bag, my first thought was "Oops, better fix this." That was Honest Gregg. Then there was "the other" Gregg, whispering in my ear. "Hey, you got away with it, it's a big store, what's the big deal?" I looked down, and there was Grandpa's money clip in my hand. That did it! I went back in and explained the mix-up. It took courage...especially since the detector buzzed on my way back in.

No gray areas

When you're honest, you're honest. There is only honest or dishonest, trustworthy or not trustworthy, no gray areas, at least for me. As Yoda in *Star Wars* put it, "Do or do not. There is no *try*." For me, there's really a very clear line about how I behave. I am truly convinced that character is founded on principles. Developing a strong character means moving away from personality, which is something entirely different. Personality in this sense means working toward being more popular and worrying about how others perceive you, which is quite different from developing a rich, deep character. When I'm working with clients or groups of people and I mention the word "character"—becoming someone who is trustworthy—what comes to mind immediately for almost everybody is their grandparents, as icons of what character means. Looking back, such principles as honesty, integrity, trust, courage and respect for the dignity of humanity seem to have come so naturally to our grandparents. Now, a generation or two later, we seem to have been taken over by a cult of personality.

Character, in the sense of moral excellence and steadfastness, is what we admire in others and hope to build in our children. Character isn't built overnight. It takes years of clear self-examination, of living every day to the best of our abilities, of aiming higher and higher. Character is built, little by little, on the solid conviction of principles.

From personality, to principles, to Love Leadership

The principles you stand for are what defines you as a leader and as an organization. I don't claim that having a principle-based platform is unique to Love Leadership, but there is an interesting progression to consider. Dale Carnegie's *How to Win Friends and Influence People*, first published in 1936, focused on developing a successful persona (the exterior), and popularized the idea of personality-based leadership. Later on, Stephen Covey added principles (the interior) to the mix of leadership skills. In fact, Covey's bestseller, *Seven Habits of Highly Effective People* (Free Press, 1989) brought principle-centered leadership to public attention, enriching and enhancing Carnegie's leadership style. My intention, with Love Leadership, is to add what I believe must become the next step in the leadership evolution: love-based leadership.

The difference between values and principles

Covey is adamant about not confusing principles and values. He proclaimed that while values govern people's behavior, it is principles that ultimately determine the consequences. Principles are external natural laws, while values are internal and subjective. Almost every corporation publishes its values. It could be a list like this:

1. Honesty and integrity
2. Teamwork
3. Entrepreneurial spirit
4. Resourcefulness
5. Dedication to community

Of these, only number one, honesty and integrity, are principles. They have a universal meaning. The others are values, which have a particular meaning for a particular company. Biker gangs, for example, can have values that aren't necessarily principles. A biker gang can believe that it's okay to stab somebody in the chest, but not okay to stab someone in the back. They might say it's okay to steal from an outsider, but not okay to steal from a gang member. Those are things they value, but it's still murder and stealing. Depending on the context, values from one person, group or company can differ radically. Principles, on the other hand, constitute the internal compass that guides you successfully through life—your true north. They must be internalized to be *your* principles; they have to be in your mind and *on* your mind. As Covey maintains, "Principles are guidelines for human conduct that are proven permanent and enduring...They're essentially unarguable because they are self-evident."

The case for principle-centered business

For almost 20 years I've been working with leaders to help identify their guiding principles, what they hold true. Starting in

---

the late 1980s, companies became infinitely more interested in determining both the values they stood for and the principles that guided their actions. The examples set in recent years by Enron and WorldComm, and numerous other companies like those two, show what happens when corporations abandon their principles. These cautionary examples have served to heighten corporate interest in reaffirming who their company is and what it (and they as people) stand for.

The art of managing people

Abigail van Buren, the renowned American newspaper advice columnist, said: "The best index to a person's character is (a) how he treats people who can't do him any good, and (b) how he treats people who can't fight back." The human element is one of the most difficult things to manage for any company or enterprise. People are not machines. Under the same organizational roof, people generally come from highly diverse backgrounds, and bring with them different perspectives. That makes it critical for any company to openly define right and wrong behavior and what principles are at its foundation, right from the start. Because if you don't, then "might" can become right, bad habits can become endemic, and morale *will* falter. It's not unlike parents teaching their children principles—if they do the job well, and live their spoken principles, rather than presenting a "Do as I say, not as I do" role model, their children have a good chance of growing up centered and well-adjusted. If not, trouble can follow—and often does.

The first step in the right direction is to define what your principles are. Ask yourself, "What do I need to start building a relationship of trust with my team?" Is it honesty, integrity, mutual respect? These are common choices, but each can also be acted on in degrees. There is a difference between being honest with someone and being *brutally* honest, just as there is a difference between trusting someone with a job and trusting them with your life. The degree of honesty or trust depends on the situation and the relationships involved. What's important is for everybody to want to adopt the principles of the group as their own.

A leader sets her company's principles in stone

Speaking of principles as an excellent tool for bringing leadership up to the next level, I am reminded again of Myrna Bentley when she became CEO of her company. As I began working with Myrna and her team, the heart and soul of that work was to first develop the principles at the foundation of the company. At the leadership and organizational level, Myrna provided her team and the company as a whole with a process for dialoguing about the principles that really mattered—not just on a business level but also on a human level. Who were they as people and as co-workers? What were the core principles of her company? What marked their path to the future? What guided their behavior as a company and as individuals in the community?

The executive team worked through this process and came up with six principles that they called "Traveling the High Road." During our discussions I had asked Myrna what was "rock solid" for them. Taking these six principles and the "solid rock" image, Myrna had the six concepts, "Honesty," "Respect," "Trust," "Compassion," "Courage" and "Integrity" carved into several sets of stones. She then gave each of her senior staff a complete set of the stones to have on their desks. Later, more people in the company received sets of the stones. After a while it became a tradition to use the stones as a kind of silent communication to trigger an important conversation or to refer to as a show of support. The process resulted in shared ownership of these six principles. As Myrna reported, "Now our corporate culture has nothing to do with who's CEO, and everything to do with how humans interact together in the organization."

I find this interesting because the principles Myrna's team came up with, such as courage and compassion, were, in my experience, pretty rare. While terms like trust and integrity often come up, courage and compassion are unusual and quite wonderful. In most companies it is about who's out front and who's ahead of whom—competitiveness. It was Myrna's Love Leadership that made it okay for fresh ideas like compassion and courage to come up and be discussed. This is important because that is what Love

Leadership is all about. It takes integrity, honesty, trust, courage, compassion, vulnerability and authenticity to lead in a Love Leadership style. And because it's not easy to live up to principles, courage and compassion are critical additions. You'll need these traits and these strengths when you're up against the inevitable adversaries and skeptics.

If you truly care about the principles, you will need to keep reinforcing them by how you behave. Myrna's leadership is one in which her organization is held accountable to its principles. It's also fundamental in this kind of leadership style to have a continuing dialogue about what the organization stands for. By having the rocks on their desks, people couldn't go through a day without thinking about them. The staff also enjoyed touching the rocks, and would pick them up and roll them in their hands while talking on the phone. There's a theory in cognitive psychology that you move toward what you think about. This is a way that Myrna's staff enriched her people and helped them build character.

The principle of compassion in action

I enjoy the magazine *Leader to Leader*. While reading the Winter 2004 issue, I came across an article by Bill George, the former chairman and CEO of Medtronic Inc. In this article he told a story about his friend Marilyn Nelson, chairman and CEO of the Carlson Companies, the privately-held hospitality and travel services giant. When she became CEO, Marilyn inherited a hard-nosed organization that, although profitable, was not known for compassion toward its employees. Shortly after assuming her new role, Marilyn had what she refers to as her "epiphany." She met with a group of MBA students who had been studying the company's culture. When she asked the students what they had discovered, no one wanted to speak. Finally, a young woman shyly raised her hand and said, "We hear from employees that Carlson is a sweatshop that doesn't care."

A good, strong leader would think, "That's incongruent with how I want to be. I want to let people *know* we care about them." Bill George said that knowing this propelled Marilyn, who *was* a good, strong leader, into taking action. She immediately created a program for employees called "Carlson Cares." Even though her staff told her they needed more time to change the company's culture, she couldn't wait. She also decided to personally become a role model for caring and empathy. As Bill George reported, "She immediately set out to change the environment, using her passion, motivational skills, and sincere interest in her employees and her customers. She took the lead on customer sales calls and interacted every day with employees in Carlson operations. Her positive energy has transformed the company's culture, built its customer relationships, accelerated its growth, and strengthened its bottom line."

Expressing his personal thoughts on the subject, Bill George went on: "Some leaders behave as though they have no compassion for anyone. It is your life experiences that open up your heart to have compassion for the most difficult challenges that people face along life's journey. Far too many leaders wall themselves off from people who are experiencing the full range of life's challenges, hardships, and difficulties. They often avoid intimate relationships, even with their friends and loved ones." Those words make me think Bill George is also an advocate of Love Leadership—even if he is not yet familiar with the term.

The principle of courage is tested

I also want to share with you a powerful story of courage and integrity that I came across in an article about trust, written by Amy Lyman, a founder and current president of the Great Place to Work® Institute (Vol. 3, Issue 1, Nov-Dec, 2003). Amy described the atmosphere of open communication and trust that was painstakingly instituted by Patrick Charmel, the president of Griffin Hospital in Derby, Connecticut. The situation was this: In November 2001, Griffin Hospital admitted the fifth patient in the nation who had inhaled anthrax. The patient subsequently died there. Charmel was put under significant pressure by high-ranking FBI officials to withhold information about the patient from his hospital staff and from the public. This was a moral dilemma for

Charmel: "Do I respect the government or my employees?" I don't know Patrick Charmel, but in this crisis, he behaved as a Love Leader. He prioritized that he had to respect his employees and went against the FBI's mandate. As Charmel explained, "I could not violate or put in jeopardy the trust relationship Griffin and I have with our employees and the community." Here's a leader whose courage also encompasses respect and integrity, and whose employees undoubtedly know that he cares about them.

An erosion of trust that goes both ways

From the beginning of time there have been many love-based, principled business owners and leaders, all over the globe. Typically, though, from the Industrial Revolution on, leadership has not involved much, if any, discussion about principles. Leadership conversations were typically about management theories and other practicalities. Perhaps leaders didn't have to worry about principles because they trusted that they could depend on ordinary people for that. Indeed, it has always been our personal principles that provide us with the common framework through which we each relate to others, and that has historically been the foundation of our communities. Interestingly though, this seems to be an area that "practical" management theory ignored, or, at best, took for granted. Companies believed they could depend on the rank-and-file's work ethic to get the job done. As a result, and for many reasons, there has been a significant erosion of trust between leadership and employees. Only principles, truly lived, can restore that mutual trust.

Valuing the message *and* the messenger

Love Leadership doesn't supplant the basic competencies you must have as a leader. You still need strong management skills in order to run a successful business. Principles are what promote and propagate a Love Leadership style throughout an organization. In the old world, bringing a behavior or action to your leader's attention put you at risk, and these fears made it virtually impossible for staff to raise issues with management. In Love Leadership, leaders want to know what their people are thinking and how they are feeling. In the old world, we cared about the message. In the new world, we also care about the person sharing the message.

Principles let your staff know what behaviors they have the right to expect from you, and what you have the right to expect from them. Expectations are clearly stated, and understood. If either party fails to live up to those expectations, a conversation is needed. In Love Leadership, behavior can always be addressed, but an individual's human dignity and humanity must always remain intact.

Respect and consideration must flow throughout the organization...like the very air you breathe.

Chapter Four

Discovering the Value of Authenticity and Vulnerability

The first rule of Love Leadership, its very foundation, is authenticity—be who you are. I had read about the importance of authenticity from several different sources. It always stuck with me that, yes, I personally want to be authentic. That said, I did not want to use authenticity as a license, as some people do, to speak "honestly," not caring if someone's feelings get hurt. That is not being authentic; it is being cruel and usually not even effective. What I have discovered is that being genuinely and effectively authentic has meant evolving into being authentically *progressive*. It's something I learned from TPI founder Lou Tice. In fact, many of my views regarding authenticity have been influenced by Lou, a man I consider my personal mentor.

In one of my first sessions with Lou, he said that there were three important things he learned when he was young: to be **authentic**, to be **progressive**, and to be **effective**. The need for authenticity is a major theme in many leadership and management styles, but with Love Leadership, it is fundamental. You simply cannot be a Love Leader without authenticity. Truly, I don't think you can be any kind of a leader without that quality, that "realness."

In the corporate world, you will find examples of companies that are pretentious in nature and those that are authentic in nature. If you work in an environment steeped in pretense, you don't know who anybody is and you don't know how anybody will react, because they react differently based on who's in the room. At an organizational level, this is costing you money.

Authenticity, like many other behavioral characteristics, begins with the leader. If a leader is authentic, it also gives his or her people permission to be authentic. For example, they would not be afraid to disagree with their boss or manager and express a contrary viewpoint. This kind of honest interaction opens the door to more meaningful dialogue, and creates the kind of honesty and clarity in discussions and decision making that can lead to better strategic planning and better short and long-term outcomes. These are concrete benefits that show up on your bottom line.

Using authenticity to smooth the road to a merger

In my consulting business, I work with many companies that are either considering a merger or already working through one. One experience stands out because of the very different personalities of the leaders of the two merging companies. One leader was nearing retirement while the other was preparing to move into position as the sole leader of the merged entity. In the interim, they were co-leading. It was an unusual arrangement, but they went about it in a positive, constructive way. I was working with both management teams, facilitating delivery of the TPI leadership curriculum. As we worked, I recognized that one team was straightforward in stating its viewpoint, while the other was more guarded, a clear reflection of their respective leaders. The older leader had a reputation for being authentic, and although he was sometimes difficult, his team always knew where they stood. Consequently, they were not afraid to question, disagree or offer suggestions to him.

The younger leader was just as effective and had equally good synergy with his team, but his approach was more guarded. The challenge was in merging these two teams under the younger man's leadership. The older leader's team, used to a more upfront approach, did not know how to approach the younger leader. In meetings I could see how much more guarded they were in their responses to him. They wondered, if they disagreed, whether that would hurt them. Would they be punished for offering alternative suggestions? Would he hold a grudge? Because they didn't know who they were dealing with, instead of being open and honest, they were pretending. This is common in any change of command, as relationships sort themselves out. But it isn't often I have the opportunity to see that clearly what a difference authenticity in a leader can make to a management team.

It's important to understand that both of these men were excellent leaders. It wasn't that one had a good personality and one did not. Personality does not make one leader good and another bad; the difference here was in how their teams interacted. With the merger, it was essential that the combined team continue to function smoothly and effectively. A major focus of the TPI curriculum is dealing with change, and, again, that requires being authentic in your dealings with others. After four days of intense work by both teams, the younger leader was left to close out the meeting. He gave a good talk, and at the end he talked about his own goals—how he felt about the company's future and why it was important to him. It was personal, touching and absolutely authentic. Afterward, the older leader's team was delighted. They finally felt they were seeing who he was and what he stood for. This allowed them to give him their support. They recognized not only his authenticity but also his vulnerability, and responded with compassion and empathy. In a nutshell, they were on his side. Isn't that what every leader wants?

Vulnerability – strength or weakness?

"Never let them see you sweat." That's a maxim we've lived with in the corporate world for countless years. For me, it falls into the old Newtonian way of doing things, when climbing the corporate ladder meant you could not, under any circumstances, show vulnerability because you would be taken advantage of, ridiculed, or considered weak. Show the other guy your weak spots and he will aim right for them. In Love Leadership, vulnerability isn't a weakness but rather a measure of the degree of trust you have in your relationships with other individuals.

Competitiveness is inherent in the human makeup, but if you don't allow yourself to be vulnerable, it means you're spending a lot of time figuring out how to hide your shortcomings instead of dealing with them. The irony is that it's quite likely that what you're trying to hide is already known.

Author Bill George sees showing your vulnerability as part of being authentic:

> *Being true to the person you were created to be means accepting your faults as well as using your strengths...I too have struggled in getting comfortable with my weaknesses—my tendency to intimidate others with an overly challenging style, my impatience, and my occasional lack of tact. Only recently have I realized that my strengths and weaknesses are two sides of the same coin. For years I felt I had to be perfect, or at least appear that I was on top of everything. I tried to hide my weaknesses from others, fearing they would reject me if they knew who I really was. Eventually, I realized that they could see my weaknesses more clearly than I could. In attempting to cover things up, I was only fooling myself...*

> *None of us is perfect, of course, but authentic leaders must have the self-discipline to do everything they can to demonstrate their values through their actions. When we fall short, it is equally important to admit our mistakes.*

Can you say "I don't know"?

Leadership is not only about knowing your vulnerabilities but being okay with showing them. One of my earlier mentors was a fellow named Jim Hutch, CEO of an influential research firm. When I met Jim, I was in my 30s, and he was nearing retirement after an illustrious career. I thought a CEO of that stature would never want to show a young up-and-comer that he didn't know everything about everything. But Jim surprised me. He was—and is—perfectly comfortable saying, "I don't know" and freely asks for opinions from those around him. That's just one of the characteristics that make me love Jim. I think my love for him is rooted in the fact that he always treated me with respect and dignity. I call that a Love Leadership style, although I don't know if Jim would. As a follower, the love I felt from him and for him unleashed in me the inspiration to be the best I could be. Sometimes I fell short. I remember one particular occasion when I was working with a board that Jim chaired. I did a PowerPoint presentation. Afterward he pulled me aside. I am a notoriously bad speller and there were mistakes in the presentation. It embarrassed Jim and he was embarrassed for me. But, as always, he looked for the good and praised me for the positive aspects before he gave me coaching on how to fix the spelling errors. That's Love Leadership.

Vulnerability means you know what your weak points are, and don't try to hide them, but rather get help or keep trying to improve. Why is that beneficial? Think about how much time we spend protecting our vulnerabilities. It's all wasted time and effort, because knowing your vulnerabilities is valuable … and not having to disguise them is liberating.

The human equation: strengths *and* weaknesses

We all have moments of strength, and moments when our strength is not evident. We also all have some areas in which we are stronger and others where we are weaker. That's natural. Practicing Love Leadership means you have the courage and honesty to uncloak both your strengths *and* your weaknesses. Being able to show your vulnerability might simply be admitting or saying out loud that you don't know the answer to a question. That gives people the confidence to say, "Hmmm, here's someone who doesn't think he's bigger or better than me—he's willing to share." That's a point of personal contact, and a fundamental piece of this whole style. In so doing, you might find that vulnerability isn't a weakness but a strength. It's also what you *do* with your vulnerability that counts. People—employees, colleagues, board members, rivals—will only perceive your vulnerability as a weakness if you allow them to.

It's like high-level team sports

When you reveal your vulnerabilities, you give others the ability to enrich you and your leadership. It allows you to bolster those areas where you're not as strong with the individual and collective strengths of your team. Doing so can profoundly benefit your performance. It's like playing high-level team sports. Recruiters do extensive scouting, carefully vetting new players to identify strengths and weaknesses. The coach then develops strategies to take advantage of a new player's strengths and compensate for any weaknesses. As a business leader, when you allow others to see your vulnerabilities, it gives your corporate team an opportunity to identify where, when and how they can compensate. It allows individual team members to see the value they bring to the table and how their skills fit into the big picture. This is the start of building personal connections with your team, making it, and the business, that much stronger.

Who needs to take the lead?

So who models this behavior first? Who demonstrates vulnerability in the corporate setting to signal that it's okay? Is it a collective leadership or a designated leader? If you have strong support people around you, they might bring the issue into the open by demonstrating their willingness to show you their vulnerability. As a leader, you might take the step because it could launch a cascade toward more open participation from your team. That momentum drives the whole notion of "free flow." Once you open up this human approach, it begins to spread to the whole team. But you have to make the decision to demonstrate vulnerability intelligently, based on your environment. It's important that you only reveal your vulnerabilities to people you trust and work closely with—you won't want to tell your competitors where your soft spots are.

The CEO as keeper of the culture

Bill Cameron, CEO and chairman of American Fidelity Assurance, a family-operated insurance company based in Oklahoma City, was featured in an article by the Great Place to Work Institute®. In it, he cited a specific situation with a person in a senior role, who was not living according to the company's values. Bill admitted that repairing the company's culture was a painful process. He held an open forum for people to come forward and talk about what happened. Bill realized that ultimately the problem was his personal responsibility, and he admitted to everyone that he should have done better. As he later explained, "I think it was a big part of our culture, when we had something like this happen, that I got up and basically apologized. Ultimately, the buck stops with me and that one got by me." This admission of vulnerability helped to rebuild credibility within the company's culture.

You may be surprised at the response

In practicing vulnerability, you discover that people rush toward you, to support you—that's the reward for allowing yourself to be human. At a workshop I was leading, a young manager with bad stage fright had to lead a one-hour session. The day of her session, she showed up with a cold and tried every escape hatch in the book before ultimately getting up. She was shaking and fighting back tears but courageously went forward. The reaction of the men and women in the room sent shivers down my spine. They rallied to her side. You could literally feel their support. They were responding at a very human level to the vulnerable spot in which she had bravely put herself. With their support, she was able to push beyond her boundaries. It wasn't just a breakthrough—it was a *bust*-through!

Another story is more personal. When my son Brogen was 14, we went kayaking with some friends. When we got out and put our boats in the water, Brogen said he was too scared to do it. He said this in front of his friend, who was younger than he was, but fearless. Brogen decided to wait with the car until we came back. We were heading out when I heard Brogen call me, "Dad, I'm going to regret this. Will you wait up?" And, despite his fear, he joined us. What moved me about this situation was not that he joined us and went kayaking, but that he had the courage to show his vulnerability, his weakness, in front of his buddy—and then the courage to confront it and challenge himself to move past his fear. He grew that day because he was prepared to make a mistake, to look stupid, to feel awkward, to be uneasy, but he was also courageous. That's the strength of showing vulnerability.

Love Leadership doesn't mean you're soft. It means you're strong enough to be open instead of closed, to consider others instead of only yourself, to be collaborative instead of controlling. Vulnerability gives something back to the people around you, who take away a deeper sense of your humanity. If you're prepared to show your vulnerability, what you get back is greater connectedness, greater sharing, and more opportunities for relationships. What you get back is more than what you disclose

> *"Whatever you do, you need courage. Whatever course you decide upon, there is always someone to tell you that you are wrong. There are always difficulties arising that tempt you to believe your critics are right. To map out a course of action and follow it to an end requires some of the same courage that a soldier needs. Peace has its victories, but it takes brave men and women to win them."*
>
> ~Ralph Waldo Emerson

Chapter Five

Courage: The Gateway to Fearlessness and Adventure

Courage makes Love Leadership possible

Courage is one of the attributes "magnetically attracted" to Love Leadership. Courage in leaders inspires courage in followers, and opens the door to adventure. Courage is both a part of and a result of Love Leadership. It takes courage to be a loving leader, and loving leadership creates courage in the folks you lead.

Courage is the glue that binds honesty, integrity, trust, respect and your other principles together. It provides the framework that guides your behavior. Think about it. If you don't have principles, what do you have to be courageous *about?* It's easier to let someone else rock the boat, to hope tough issues resolve themselves. But in truth, they don't. That's the crux of the matter and why you need courage to be a Love Leader.

Failing to act with courage has consequences

Love Leaders look for and identify their own mistakes. Courageous leadership is not just for crisis situations; it is how you live and work every day. You know that, as a leader, when you do not address situations, you will invariably face unpleasant human resources and bottom line consequences. Productivity, efficiency, teamwork, synergy and creativity are all negatively impacted when leaders fail to act with courage. It is courage that lets you address challenges, and courage that opens the gates to greater levels of success.

A client of mine leads a business that has grown from a small enterprise into a large, successful company. One day he called to ask for my help in dealing with a growing morale problem. As we explored the situation, the source of the problem became clear. One of his long-time employees was a volatile manager who would periodically blow up and scream at his staff, embarrassing and humiliating them. The people at the receiving end of this were courageous enough to reveal the source of their low morale. My client's response was, "Oh, that's just Ted. He's always been that way and it always blows over. Don't pay any attention." Well, the staff *did* pay attention, they did notice, and they did feel it.

My client just didn't have the courage to deal with the issue, partly because Ted was good at his job and got results. I challenged my client to consider the hidden costs. How many good employees had he lost? What was his turnover, his retraining costs, his productivity losses? And what were the chances of his employees ever taking a risk and going above and beyond bare minimum requirements to do their jobs under this man? Some leaders turn a blind eye to abusive behavior because the abuser is also a producer. That's avoidance and fearfulness, and it will cost you in the end, just as it cost my client. In a Love Leadership style, your concern for the rest of your team gives you the courage to talk to an abusive team member, and, if the behavior does not improve, to terminate him. By doing nothing about this behavior, not openly rejecting it, you are actually *accepting* it. You don't have to be angry or cold-hearted to fire someone, but you do need the courage to see and act clearly in the best interests of all concerned.

A lesson from the United States Air Force

The U.S.A.F. Blue Angels aerobatics team has a catch-phrase: "Fess up and fix it." In point of fact, this team spends twice as much time debriefing *after* a flight as they do briefing before it. They go back over every performance and every maneuver to identify what could have been improved. Rather than remaining overlooked or hidden, any mistakes are openly recognized and addressed. "Fess up and fix it" is about accountability—and about courage. These pilots can be courageous in owning up to and dissecting their mistakes because their dignity and honor are not at risk, and neither are their jobs. The door is open to owning mistakes because the focus is not on punishment but on solutions—yet another good reason for every company to have a Love Leadership culture in place.

Move this into a corporate setting. If your employees are worried about getting chewed out, they will creatively avoid confrontation and hide any information about how something happened that shouldn't have. They won't fess up and it won't get fixed. Leading in a Love Leadership style lets you create an environment that accepts mistakes—and demands accountability. As you create this style, you lead the way for others to develop the same courageous style. It is inherently entrepreneurial. Entrepreneurs are not fearful avoiders who do only what they are asked; they are fearless risk-takers who speak candidly and challenge each other. These are the qualities that build high performance teams who can not only meet but also exceed goals and requirements.

The negative power of fear

When my son was younger, I helped coached his basketball team. The head coach had a distinctive style. If a kid didn't do what was asked or made a mistake, he held them accountable. That seemed good—in theory. Then I noticed something that wasn't so good. The kids had become fearful of making mistakes. Instead of owning up to mistakes, they avoided addressing them, hoping nobody would notice. They also started to point out mistakes other boys made as a way to avoid being singled out. The kids weren't responding to this leadership style with courage, but with fear. This is actually a classic pattern of human behavior. When you're fearful and worried about being caught, you become an ally of the leader you're afraid of, and try to catch other people doing the very thing you're afraid of being caught doing.

The same thing happens in organizations. Whether coaching a Little League team or a high performance business team, the leader who tries to motivate through fear of consequences is missing the bigger picture—not seeing the negative power of fear and its damaging consequences. Using fear as motivator creates a "do-it-or-else" scenario. As soon as you put something on an "or else" basis, you'll find that when the task becomes too hard, people quit. Human beings need to be internally motivated in order to overcome obstacles and reach higher, and this can't come from fear. Good leaders, coaches and teachers understand this.

This quote attributed to Mahatma Gandhi gets to the heart of what I'm saying: *"Power is of two kinds. One is obtained by the fear of punishment, and the other by acts of love. Power based on love is a thousand times more effective and permanent than the one derived from fear of punishment."* When people know you truly care about them as individuals, it seems to release them from fear. This release allows people to be fearless in their approach to the future—they can go forward with courage and the desire to achieve. They know that if they make a mistake, it will be acknowledged and discussed but not punished. And that opens their minds to look at opportunities with a sense of adventure rather than avoidance.

The courage of Love Leadership overcomes fear

I think this little story illustrates the connection between demonstrating courage and creating a climate of fearlessness and adventure. My good friend Dave and I were invited to coach the freshmen boy's basketball team at our local high school. We spent a good deal of time talking about how we were going to approach the season, in terms of strategy and what we wanted to achieve. We were committed to developing not just strong ballplayers but also good young men. With this in mind, when we held the first try-outs, we were thoughtful about our comments and sensitive toward the boys' self-esteem, which at 14 and 15 can be fragile. As head coach, Dave took a leadership role in developing our assessment methods and providing feedback. During the assessment process, we kept in mind our original goal, which was to accommodate as many kids as possible who could play at a certain level.

In the end, there were only four kids who didn't meet that skills level. Dave and I had several conversations about what to do. Finally, we realized we weren't doing anyone any favors trying to include every boy. We had to face it; four kids just didn't make the grade. I was feeling really awkward about having to cut these four teens. To be honest, I was fearful of hurting them. Dave took each boy aside. Because he is a Love Leader, the way he gave them the news was aligned with his commitment to protect their dignity and self-esteem.

The telling part of the story is that after they were cut, two of the four boys e-mailed both Dave and me to say how much they had appreciated the opportunity to try out. Three of the four still wanted to be on the practice team, even though they wouldn't be playing in any games. Dave's courage in dealing with the boys in a way that protected their dignity and confidence created a sense of fearlessness and adventure, which gave the boys the courage to continue to participate and contribute in a different way. It also showed me that I still had work to do to act with courage.

This is a different approach than the more common "tough luck" attitude, and I think the results speak for themselves. Now take this into an organizational setting—having to terminate someone, for example. If you can do something difficult like that while protecting the dignity of the individual, chances are you'll create something positive, or at least lessen the negative impact.

Love trumps fear

When my nephew Fergie was six or seven, he won a pair of pig slippers in a little contest. Boy, did that young man love those slippers! He wore them everywhere. But when he wanted to wear them to school, his mother, my sister Jody, put her foot down. She was afraid he would be laughed at, and wanted to protect him. Well, he wore them anyway. When she picked him up after school, she was pretty sure she was going to have to do some damage control. To her surprise, Fergie hopped in the car with the same enthusiasm and smile he had when he left that morning. When Jody asked him how school was, he said cheerfully, "Oh, I got laughed at." And that was it—he was fine. It didn't matter that the other kids laughed at him—his love of those pig slippers outweighed any embarrassment.

A while back I was asked to play my guitar at a friend's retirement party. I'm not comfortable performing, but Barry is a good friend, so I agreed. When I got there, the microphone was all set up and Barry asked me to play and *sing* in front of that room full of people. Now I was *really* uncomfortable. I really did not want to stand up in front of a crowd and sing. Did I do it anyway? Yeah. Would I do it again? Yeah, because I love Barry.

My point is that if love is more important, your fear of embarrassment or failure is lessened. Love simply outweighs those things. The love my nephew had for his pig slippers outweighed the teasing he knew he would be in for at school. The love I had for my friend Barry was greater than my fear of embarrassing myself in front of all those people. That's freedom.

Failure vs. Mistakes

I was coaching a friend of mine who had recently taken on a leadership role within his organization. At one point I said to him, "I never fail." This is actually one of my affirmations, but the statement struck him as being arrogant and bold. That led to a dialogue on failure versus mistakes. It didn't take long before he reached the same conclusion as I had. Yes, we all make mistakes; it's part of the learning process. But making a mistake is not failing. Lou Tice has an e-mail subscription he offers called Winner's Circle. In one called "It's Only Failure If You Think It Is" Lou wrote: "Edison tried thousands of different materials before he found the right filament for the electric light bulb. When asked why he didn't quit, he said,

'Why should I? I now know 2,000 things that don't work!' If you look at your experiences the way Edison did, you are much more likely to achieve success." You only fail at something if you lack the courage to continue or tried something that didn't work the way you expected and don't take something positive away from the experience.

About a week later I happened to be sitting beside the fax machine as a fax was coming out. It read:

PAGE 1 OF 1

TO: Gregg Cochlan

Gregg:
I only made four mistakes this week.
I will try harder next week.

Kieron

It's okay to make mistakes

At the time, I was not yet clear on Love Leadership, but I was clear on the notion that if you can create a belief in people that mistakes are okay, they stop worrying about failure and their performance improves. As a Love Leader, you are better able to develop this fearlessness in people because they know they are loved. That's a basic premise of Love Leadership. A safe environment means it is okay to make mistakes and even to fall short of goals. But, let me be clear, although Love Leadership accepts mistakes, it does not let people off the hook. In fact, you never provide an escape hatch for people to be less than they could be. You just never use failure as a weapon.

I don't get it. Why do we expect employees to enhance their performance with a gun to their heads? Does that make sense to you? I know from my own experience that the "stick approach" can get results, but ask yourself how much greater those results would be if employees felt secure and valued enough to really tap into their potential? Love Leadership can take you—and others who look to you for guidance—to this higher level.

Love Leaders throw their people out of order

In some ways, Love Leadership is more rigorous than a command-and-control or decide-and-announce style of leadership. To show the contrast, Love Leadership is rooted in a personal belief system that impels you to want to see people live up to their potential. Most of us want to live up to our potential, even if not all of us have the confidence, self-esteem or discipline to try. Love Leaders constantly challenge people to live up to their abilities. Some of the best leaders I have worked for, or teachers I have learned from, had the courage to challenge me and "throw me out of order."

One of my first presentations, back in the late 80s, was to our senior management team at SaskTel. Gord Farmer, the General Manager, challenged me to develop a PowerPoint presentation to help explain my position on "Excellent Customer Service." With a fair amount of discomfort, I did so and presented my thoughts. The good news was that the attendees accepted my position. The bad news is that it took me 105 slides to tell them. When I look back, Gord sure threw me out of order, but I learned and improved a great deal from doing that one presentation. Love Leaders are more than prepared to throw their people out of order. But they are also respectful and know how far they can throw them. Gord had set me up to be successful. From this experience, Gord also earned my steadfast respect. I knew I would never want to let him down, and I never did. The best leaders are never pushovers—they stand their ground and challenge their people to do their very best. As Lou Tice says, *"You need to let people know that while it is okay to fall down, it is not okay to stay down."*

High expectations without the human cost

Let me define what I mean by high expectations. Over the years, I have worked with executive and management teams who believe that "high expectations" means working weekends, nights and always being on call, even during vacation time. It is the old-fashioned expectation of "do or die trying" and it does not include any sense of caring about the individual. Again, I am not saying this isn't effective; I know from my own experience that it can be. My argument is that Love Leadership gets the same result without the human cost.

Love Leadership maximizes the potential of your employees and team members. They live up to your expectations because they begin to have those expectations of themselves. In my experience, when leaders stop viewing people as disposable, they are rewarded with elevated effort, enhanced performance, more creative thinking, more flexibility and greater adaptability to change. As an employee, when you know your employer cares about you as a person and not just as intellectual capital, you care more about your employer. The same holds true for members of project or management teams. The upshot is that when your team leader or boss has a problem, so do you. You no longer give up accountability for success; you take a share in it.

Thinking of work as a game adds an element of fun

When I read Charles Coonradt's *The Game of Work*, two things struck me. First, I loved the idea that you can treat work as a game. That makes sense to me. The second was the "have to" versus "want to" perspective. Sure, work matters, but my real life is my family. When I totally accepted that mindset, I moved work away from the fear-based "I have to do well" into a fearless "want to" adventure. Tasks and projects became less onerous and more fun. This neatly fit with my own evolving leadership style. Knitting some of these perspectives together with The Pacific Institute education, I began not only to think of work as a game, but also to look at the behavior of those I was leading in a much different way. When someone on my team was behaving inconsistently, or not performing up to par, instead of judging the behavior, I became curious about the motivation behind it. In this, The Pacific Institute education has proved especially valuable. If you become judgmental, you tend to lock onto one point of view and lock out all other options. By supplanting judgment with inquisitiveness, you can dig deeper and allow yourself the opportunity to see the big picture rather than a focused snapshot—which leads to better decision making.

Love Leadership as an awfully big adventure

One of my clients is a young CEO who has already been through six mergers, two amalgamations and two major technology implementations. When I heard that, I said, "Wow! What a great adventure you're on!" I didn't have to convince him; he readily affirmed it. He saw his position as an exciting journey filled with opportunities. That's the new normal. Ten years ago, most business leaders were just running their companies; now they're navigating change at an unprecedented rate, often with courage and enthusiasm.

Since Love Leadership has courage as one of its essential attributes, it opens up the door to adventure. "Adventure" is defined in the dictionary as:

> **ad·ven·ture** *noun*
> 1: an exciting or extraordinary event or series of events, 2: an undertaking involving uncertainty and risk and 3: the participation or willingness to participate in things that involve uncertainty and risk.

To my mind, that's also the definition of a team imbued with courage and fearlessness. Your courage as a leader can turn your staff into an adventurous group of explorers who are willing to accept, tackle and embrace change.

A group of people willing to take on anything

Work can become a productive game when you help your people stop resisting change. Instead of moaning and groaning about change, they will welcome it with a "bring it on" enthusiasm. As each obstacle is overcome, the new ones don't look so big and scary. There's an old saying that obstacles always seem bigger when they're in front of you, and practically insignificant when they're behind you.

The more challenges your team faces, the more adept they become at figuring out how to clear hurdles and move projects forward. And that is, or should be, exactly who you want at your side—a group of people willing to take on anything. As a courageous, adventurous Love Leader, you will have inspired an environment where people can fall down, but they don't stay down. This is where you start to see accelerated confidence and, as a result, accelerated performance.

People are at their best if they are not limited by judgment. They are fearless. When your team can perform without fear, their creativity and innovation grow exponentially. When your team feels safe in being who they are, without pretense, their overall performance will soar and their accomplishments will continue to multiply.

> *"I have never met a person whose greatest need was anything other than real, unconditional love. You can find it in a simple act of kindness toward someone who needs help. There is no mistaking love. You feel it in your heart. It is the common fiber of life, the flame that heats our soul, energizes our spirit and supplies passion to our lives."*
> ~Elisabeth Kubler-Ross

Chapter Six

Good Beyond Self: The Deepest Meaning of Love

Friends and heroes

We all have heroes in our lives and Dennis Lyster is one of mine. He died in 2004 after a four-year adventure with cancer. Even in the middle of his grave illness, Dennis never stopped thinking of others. Throughout this time, he modeled a Love Leadership style that was truly good beyond self, which is the subject of this chapter. This is an e-mail I received from Dennis in 2003.

———Original Message———
From: Dennis Lyster
Sent: Mon Oct 20 17:56:26 2003
Subject: Hey

Sorry I missed your call today. I would have enjoyed a visit with you. I was scrambling to tidy things up this p.m. both with CT and Catholic Family Services that my time did not fit into your available time.

I start my treatment stuff tomorrow. Get a PICC line installed at St. Paul's tomorrow morning (intravenous line that goes into a vein in your arm and ends just at the start of your heart). This takes a couple of hours and then allows many functions without continually jabbing you with a needle. Primary purpose is to inject chemo mix into my blood system so that it gets into all the areas of my body to kill or shrink cancer cells.

Wednesday I will spend most of the day at the Cancer Center having my first treatment. I know that everything will go well so I can make the Board Executive Committee on Thursday.

Thanks for keeping in touch and I want to especially thank you for the journal you gave me. I wanted to save it for a special purpose and it is now my day to day record of my life, feelings and emotions. My affirmations are all recorded in my brain. I have a hard time getting these to be personal and find that they are for family and friends and colleagues, that's just the way I am.

My illness is affecting those around me to a greater degree than myself. It is kind of like I'm sitting outside of this situation and looking in at all these folks that are hurting for me and I feel so bad that I am hurting them so much. My mother, Yvette, the boys, my close friends and all those people that care do not desire this burden. It is not fair for them.

—End of Message—

Even in the midst of his battle, this brave, humble "warrior" was committed to easing the pain of those around him, rather than focusing solely on himself. While he ultimately lost the battle, he won the war...he will long be remembered lovingly by those whose lives he touched and inspired.

A foundation of leadership

"Good beyond self" is one of four levels of happiness that Dr. Robert J. Spitzer talks about in his book *The Spirit of Leadership*. Happiness level one, or H1, is immediate gratification; H2 is ego gratification; H3 is good beyond self. I believe that human beings naturally evolve throughout our lives. We mature from immediate gratification to ego gratification to good beyond self. When we reach the point in the continuum where we recognize that there are things more important than ourselves, we find our greatest rewards in giving rather than in getting. Of course, the great thing about giving love is that you get love back.

As leaders, we follow the same process. We evolve from wanting the immediate gratification of doing a job well and the ego gratification of having others recognize we are doing the job well, to wanting to lead and guide others, so that they too can do the job well and garner the resulting satisfaction and sense of significance. This, to me, is level H3 or good beyond self. It's something of an intangible, but, like parenting or friendship, it is one of the things that matters the most. And it's about what you do, not just what you say.

At this point in my life, my overriding goal is to increase my capacity for love. I mentioned earlier that when I started writing this book, I searched for another word besides "love." Now, in telling you about the concept of "good beyond self," I feel the need again. In my ongoing research within this area, I read two marvelous books that discussed the four words for love used by the ancient Greeks to distinguish the different types of love from each other. Those books were *The Spirit of Leadership: Optimizing Creativity and Change in Organizations* (Executive Excellence Publishing, 2000) by Dr. Spitzer, and *The Four Loves* by C. S. Lewis (Harcourt, Brace and Company, 1960). Dr. Spitzer used the English renditions of the Greek words, *Storge, Philia, Eros* and *Agape*. C.S. Lewis used English words for these four kinds of love: Affection, Friendship, Eros, and Charity, respectively. Lewis also discusses them in terms of "Need-Love" and "Gift-Love."

As Dr. Spitzer explained, storge [STOR' gay] is the affection we feel for others toward whom we feel natural affinity, such as the love of parents for children and vice versa. *Philia* is friendship that goes beyond affection, one based on mutual interests. The more mutual interest and concern there is, the deeper the friendship and the longer the commitment is likely to be. Friendships grow as care is extended, accepted, and reciprocally given in return. So long as the reciprocity is maintained, friendship continues and grows. *Eros* is romantic love, motivated by feelings of intimacy and care for the other in ways that lead to exclusive mutual commitment. *Agape* is the deepest love. Dr. Spitzer calls it "the care for another motivated solely by an awareness of the intrinsic dignity of that other." As he explains, "It need not be supported by feelings of affection (*storge*), or by the promise of reciprocity (*philia*), or feelings of intimacy or romance (*eros*). Agape arises out of a call to serve the intrinsically dignified other. The emotion accompanying the other three kinds of love may complement agape, but agape does not need them. *This purest form of love must be motivated out of a deep, transparent vision of the intrinsic dignity of the other*, or by faith and prayer." [emphasis added]

C.S. Lewis' book points out the distortions that can take place, particularly in Affection and Friendship. Affection can become demanding, placing a burden upon the beloved, like the mother who makes her children feel an unrelieved guilt. Friendships can arise from mutual interest among criminals. True Eros is purer because it involves devotion, with sexual desire more an outcome than a basis for that kind of love. And, to Lewis, Charity is love like the love of God, the love that raises the quality of the other three. It is devoid of judgment or a need for recognition or reciprocity. "Charity" is the translation of the Greek word *agape* used in the St. James version of the Bible, most notably in 1 Corinthians, Chapter 13, which begins "Though I speak with the tongues of men and of angels, and have not charity, I am become as sounding brass, or a tinkling cymbal."

Why good beyond self may work miracles

As Dr. Spitzer claims, "Agape is worth pursuing in and of itself. It is also one of the most effective leadership tools imaginable." I agree. Agape is the love of good beyond self, and it is astonishingly powerful. One of Lou Tice's friends, Matthew Budd, a former professor at the Harvard University School of Medicine, told us about a colleague of his who was interested in finding out if people could improve their health just by looking at random acts of kindness. Could greater health and strength be created for someone undergoing a surgical operation, for example, if they watched random acts of kindness beforehand?

That was back in the 1970s. The colleague that Professor Budd referred to was David McClelland, who was then a Harvard psychology professor. McClelland was engaged in researching how people could improve the functioning of their immune systems. As part of his research, he showed his students films of Mother Teresa helping babies. He wanted to see if these films could evoke feelings of caring and loving, and if those feelings produced positive effects on the immune system. To determine if it did, he measured the amount of immunoglobulin A (part of the body's defense against cold viruses) in saliva before and after people viewed these films. What he found was that their immune systems strengthened, regardless of whether or not they admired Mother Teresa's work. McClelland also discovered that the students with the most beneficial immune-system results were not those who were motivated simply by a desire to connect with others. Instead, those who wanted to do something positive for, with, or involving another person without regard for the outcome—in other words, to achieve what I call "good beyond self."

McClelland and his fellow researchers called this an "affiliative connection"—a relationship of friendship, love, or some sort of positive bonding, concluding that these altruistic emotions can affect the immune system. Further studies by others at Harvard seemed to confirm this conclusion; students who showed more affiliative trust had greater helper-to-suppressor T-cell ratios, another immunity parameter that indicates our ability to resist disease. Finally, McClelland reported, "We have preliminary evidence in a longitudinal study that people who are high in Affiliative Trust show fewer instances of major illnesses nine years after the assessment." From this it appears clear that helping others is a good way to not only build trust and connection, but is another way to add to our own personal protection against disease. Others have reported that acting from good beyond self increases our level of happiness. Here is an indication that Love Leadership can also improve our health, and that the rewards of Love Leadership are, literally, endless.

After I heard about this research, I gave a keynote speech on random acts of kindness. I challenged the audience to give some of their time to doing random acts of kindness. Given the fact that their employer was giving them this very afternoon off, I suggested they go do some good work later that day to get first-hand experience of "good beyond self." As it happened, 85 percent of those 1,500 people did go out and perform random acts of kindness. The immediate scene that stuck in my mind was seeing two employees almost fighting each other to open a door for an elderly lady who was struggling to open it. The feedback I got was overwhelmingly positive from both the givers and receivers. Most interestingly, at first they had to be conscious of doing kindnesses, but after a while this mindset began to "set in" and became a part of who they were, rather than a conscious effort.

There is the known payoff of good-beyond-self behavior and thinking, although, in my experience, the reward is usually not immediate. Good beyond self leads to intangible rewards, much like parenting. The countless things parents do for their children are selfless acts. They do them for the greater good of their children, who usually aren't even aware of them until they themselves begin to mature. In a similar way, leaders do things for the greater good of the people around them—their teams, their customers, their communities. It's an intrinsic part of a giving style of leadership. That's the fit with Love Leadership. Love Leaders look at how their actions benefit, support or enable their team members to achieve their goals. How far would that go? Let's say an employee's family has been devastated by a fire. A Love Leader would look for ways to support the recovery of that family—even to the point of providing resources out of the company's funds or out of his or her own pocket—another example of good beyond oneself.

Why good beyond self is not a result of knowledge or age

While I do believe we are all on an evolutionary path, I no longer believe good beyond self automatically comes with age and maturity. One of my turning points was a story I heard on CBC Radio, the Canadian national public broadcasting company. Ryan Hreljac was a six-year-old boy in a small town in Ontario, Canada. His first grade teacher told his class that children in Africa had to walk miles to get a drink of water and that many children got sick and died from drinking bad water. The school was raising money for African relief and Ryan learned that $70 could help a village in Africa get a well. Somehow, this idea really took root with the boy. It took him four months of doing chores to raise the $70, but when he took the money in, he learned that $70 was not enough. That would buy a hand pump, but a well actually cost $2,000. That would put a lot of kids off—but not this boy. He went back and raised all the necessary money. With adult help, Ryan went on to establish the Ryan's Well Foundation, which to date has raised more than $1.5 million and built 255 wells that now serve more than 427,000 people in 12 countries. That's neither immediate gratification nor ego gratification. It's good beyond self. And it shows you don't have to be 50 or 75 years old to achieve it.

Another astonishing good beyond self, agape love story

Shortly before ten o'clock on the morning of October 2, 2006, a 32-year-old milk truck driver, armed with three guns, took ten Amish schoolgirls hostage in a small Pennsylvania community. By the time police arrived, this man had killed three of the girls and himself. Two more girls later died of their wounds, and a sixth girl, only six years old, was still comatose six months later. Unbelievably, before that devastating day had ended, the Amish community had sent a message of forgiveness to the gunman's wife and family. Later, the fathers of the slain girls even offered help and comfort to the killer's parents. This is a true example of their capacity to love—to have the conviction to show love under the most difficult circumstances. For most of us, it's inconceivable. This is the love the Greeks called agape, and demonstrates the epitome of good beyond self.

I don't know what has since happened to this aggrieved family, but I believe that the killer's parents and his wife and children have a far better chance of moving forward in their own lives than they would have had without this loving gesture on the part of the Amish. Instead of feeling shame and hiding themselves, they might even feel empowered to go and speak to people about how their family member lost his mind. They might feel so vested in the relationship that they might partner with the Amish to do presentations on how to recognize mental illness. This kind of outreach might help motivate others to become more forgiving, and turn tragedy into a way to make the world a better place.

I'm not sure if I could ever be that extraordinarily forgiving if it were my children who were killed, but it does make me want to try harder to extend my hand first. Certainly, the way that the Amish reacted made me want to look for ways to diminish my occasional bouts of anger, frustration or conflicts with people. Given this *extreme* example, employing love beyond self to help us overcome conflict in the workplace with our employees, our coworkers and our teams should be relatively easy to accomplish.

Good beyond self as an intrinsic part of human nature

I don't believe you can truly evolve a Love Leadership style without having the intent of doing acts for the greater good. It's an awakening in which you realize what really matters to you, and a realization that doing something that creates more benefit than you'll actually receive *is* personally rewarding. Good beyond self is the primal foundation on which Love Leadership stands. C. S. Lewis further described agape as Divine Love and also as divine energy where "there is no hunger that needs to be filled, only plenteousness that desires to give." The love in Love Leadership is this same expansive, divine *energy* that continuously draws abundance. Mother Teresa said, "There is more hunger for love and appreciation in this world than for bread."

Abundance versus scarcity

Many stories of "abundance versus scarcity" have a Biblical origin. I am not a religious person, but many wonderful people I know are, and there are powerful points to be made in holy texts. The Book of Genesis, for example, starts out with a liturgy of abundance in the story of creation. Psalm 104: 24 proclaims: "O Lord, how manifold are thy works! In wisdom hast thou made them all: the earth is full of thy riches." In Exodus, manna is seen to fall from heaven. In the Gospel of John, Jesus performs his first miracle by turning water into wine. The story of a few loaves and fishes feeding five thousand people comes from Mark. Interestingly, each of these stories or parables starts with the fear of scarcity. The two ideas compose opposite mindsets that engender emotions that can direct the way we approach problems and challenges in all our dealings with other people.

In the scarcity mindset, we think competition is the source of survival—i.e., beating out the other guy for the goods. If you think there's not enough of something to go around, you can't evolve beyond a need for immediate gratification because you're too busy trying to meet your own needs. In a scarcity mindset everything is seen as finite, limited, scarce. In this "reality" you only have so much to give, whether it's time, money or love. You guard what you have and limit disbursements of your time, money or love to yourself and your immediate family. Ironically, instead of feeling you have enough, you find you have less and less of what you need, and become filled with fear about the future and afraid of anyone you believe might take away what little you have. Scarcity inspires self-doubt and despair. This perception then leads to suspicion, judging others and holding grudges, which leads to anger and attacking behavior.

A scarcity mentality in the corporate world says there's only so much to go around—finite opportunities. If you take one, there's less for me. If I want more, I have to take it from you. Now this might have some of you wondering if this means we should be less prudent or circumspect with budget deliberations. Does this mean there may be a slackening of fiscal responsibility, and in its place a more freewheeling, risky way of behaving? Not at all. Leaders absolutely need to manage their company or organization's bottom line, and there are always some limitations on a budget, just as there are limitations on everything. My point is that Love Leaders look at the world from a perspective of abundance, not scarcity, and always work toward encouraging others to do the same.

How an abundance mentality leads to more abundance

A feeling of abundance—that the Universe is a place of abundance, that there is more than enough for everyone—takes away limitations. This kind of thinking inspires cooperation and sharing instead of fear. An abundance mindset also creates feelings of interdependence, safety and love. Because you feel safe, you are full of forgiveness, which leads to freedom. This freedom is an atmosphere that engenders creativity, risk-taking and adventure. In this state, there is no failure, only learning—even when expensive mistakes are made. Also, forgiving others allows you to forgive yourself, which leads to serenity, joy, generous behavior, and giving of yourself. These are the essence of good beyond self, a capacity that the fearful, scarcity mindset can never reach.

As I have become more of a Love Leader I find my ability to look at the world in terms of abundance increasing in noticeable ways. I can see it in my ability to not hold grudges, to forgive, to appreciate the good things in people. This was driven home to me one day when I was talking with my son Brogen.

"Who are your best friends?" he asked.

"Al is one," I said.

"Do you love him?"

"Yeah."

"Are there things that bug you about him?"

"No."

"Who else?"

"Eldon."

"What bugs you about him?"

"Nothing."

This little exchange got me thinking. I went through a mental inventory of the people I'm close to and found my capacity to appreciate their good qualities outweighed any faults I also thought they might have. The realization I arrived at was that there is no limit to my capacity to love. At some point in my life I would have reserved the love I have just to my immediate family. But now, as I mature, my capacity to love has increased. There isn't a scarcity of love—there is an abundance of love.

Let's look at the abundance/scarcity paradigm in a given company from a Love Leadership perspective. In a scarcity model, you would concentrate your time, attention and energy on a few favorites. This might be great for the chosen few, but what does it say to everyone else on your team? Compare the productivity level, morale and performance of your favorites and non-favorites. An abundance model lets you spend time, attention and energy on *every* member of your team.

It is also important to include "time" in this picture, because time is one of the resources we typically consider to be in short supply. If you can instill a sense of abundance in your organization, which includes helping them intelligently reapportion their time so that they do not always feel "time-starved," you free your people, allowing them to be less afraid and become more adventurous. Seeing abundance everywhere—of time, of energy, of goodwill, of resources—will soon become contagious. Once experienced, who would not favor this attitude over a scarcity mindset?

I have no doubt whatsoever that a culture of abundance, coming from the top down, and embraced by everyone, is absolutely essential to the ultimate success of any company, organization or enterprise. Skeptics may very well dismiss my stance as utopian or see me as a Pollyanna, citing all of the tragic, destructive, hateful occurrences in the world. How, they might ask, could the war-torn, starving, homeless mothers and children in Africa profit from an abundance mentality? I'm not claiming foreign policy expertise, but consider this: the prosperous nations of this planet could eliminate poverty if they wanted to. I will go even further: *An attitude of abundance, coupled with love that seeks good beyond self can, I believe, change the world.*

> "In these troubled, uncertain times, we don't need more command and control: we need better means to engage everyone's intelligence in solving challenges and crises as they arise."
>
> ~Margaret J. Wheatley

Chapter Seven

The Importance of Followership

9/11 ushers in a whole new world

"Love in organizations is the most potent source of power we have available," Margaret Wheatley wrote in her groundbreaking 1992 book, *Leadership and the New Science*, which became a bestseller and is now in its third revised edition. In an interview just weeks after the attacks on the World Trade Center, Wheatley said she believed the event had a powerful impact on notions of leadership. A question we need to ask ourselves, she said, is this: "What is the leadership the world needs now and what are we learning about leadership from actually being followers?" Wheatley maintained that we had witnessed the failure of the secretive, command-and-control kind of leadership, and must fundamentally shift our ideas about leading and following. "I believe on September 11th there were numerous corporate leaders who suddenly realized that people really were the most important thing to them, even though an hour before they'd been working a system that ignored human concerns," she said. It is a shame that, for many of us, it took an event like 9/11 to bring humanity into sharper focus. What is even more shameful is that this tragic event did not, for the most part, really create sustainable change.

Wheatley went on to explain that control is an illusion and emphasized the importance of leadership that trusts and empowers followers:

I think it will take a little while for Americans to really accept that there is no control possible in this greater interconnected world...One of the great ironies right now is that no matter how good you were as a business before September 11th and no matter how skilled you were at planning, and no matter how skilled you were at budgeting, everything's shifted. The only way to lead when you don't have control is you lead through the power of your relationships. You can deal with the unknown only if you have enormous levels of trust, and if you're working together and bringing out the best in people.

Why leaders are defined by followership

Leaders need willing followers or they're just dictators. I love the word *followership*. It's not something I invented—it's been around for half a century at least, although it was not in Webster's Dictionary that entire time. You might think that "followership" is the opposite of leadership. After all, we think of followers as subordinates, underlings. They're the ones taking orders, aren't they? They're the meek and mild, the enlisted man saluting the officer. But there's a difference between someone who is just working for a paycheck and a follower. Followers are *participants*. They are not just passengers along for the ride; they participate in the journey. In this way, the role of a follower actually resembles that of a leader.

The integral relationship that exists between leaders and followers was clarified for me by Ira Chaleff in his book, *The Courageous Follower*. As Chaleff explained, sometimes it is followers who provide leadership. A good follower has, first and foremost, a willingness to tell the truth. Great followership is having the courage and compassion to bring something to the attention of the leader. Leaders depend on their people for accurate and timely information, whether or not it is something they want to hear. Followers also must have the courage to speak up. They may feel uncomfortable communicating honestly with the leader, but at the same time they realize that they can and must play a decisive role in helping the leader make better decisions. Having the courage to speak honestly is a leadership trait. In my experience, successful leaders accomplish what they do because of great followership. As Robert Greenleaf, founder of the Servant Leadership movement, which encourages collaboration, trust, foresight, listening, and the ethical use of power and empowerment, said, "The only test of leadership is that somebody follows."

In an environment where Love Leadership predominates, people will develop strong followership. And they won't just follow; they will be prepared and willing to challenge leaders. One of the unique characteristics of Love Leadership is that it *wants* followers to challenge assumptions and beliefs—yours, theirs and others. I've seen this in operation. I work with a number of executive teams and I'm always interested in the dynamics of the individuals involved. In one instance, two senior staff pulled me aside after a session to share their concern about their CEO's performance. I pressed them a little, trying to find out what this was about. I wondered if they were trying to get the fellow fired. I asked if his performance was affecting the company, and they admitted they thought it was. So I asked them if they were jeopardizing the company by not going to the Board of Directors with their concerns. They became upset at this suggestion. They absolutely did *not* want to get him fired; they wanted to help him find a way to improve his performance. They saw him faltering and wanted to do something. In this, they were being good followers. Shortly after this conversation, one of them did have a frank conversation with the CEO and candidly told him his viewpoint. His comments were received by the CEO with grace and respect.

To quote leadership studies pioneer Warren Bennis, "Good

leaders make people feel that they're at the very heart of things, not at the periphery. Everyone feels that he or she makes a difference to the success of the organization. When that happens people feel centered and that gives their work meaning."

Followership and understanding *why* we work

Followership is linked to motivation. Why *do* people work? You might say that we work to put food on the table and a roof over our heads. While that is true, it hardly explains it all. One of the things that many people get wrong about Love Leadership is that they assume it means paying higher salaries and more generous pensions, with some employers also providing such amenities as free food and transportation, a free gym membership, allowing people to choose the hours they want to work, and assuring them their jobs are so secure that they will never get laid off. In fact, Love Leadership is not about any of these things. Certainly, a Love Leader might want to provide some of these benefits to employees, but you can still be a Love Leader without any of these perks.

In his book *Even Eagles Need a Push: Learning to Soar in a Changing World*, David McNally describes three reasons why people work: money, affiliation and meaning. "Meaning" is subjective, including things like personal satisfaction, a sense of purpose, happiness, enabling others to make a difference, and service. "Affiliation" is one's sense of being part of a group, team or community, and incorporates ideas like shared success, support, development, a sense of belonging, connection. Within affiliation is responsibility—being part of a bigger whole, a co-builder, if you will, of organizations and self-concepts. Finally, there's money. Money, in actuality, meets the lower level needs that we all have, such as food and shelter. Money is an extrinsic basic motivator. Love Leadership creates intrinsic values in the areas of both affiliation and meaning.

The superior value of intrinsic motivation

Love Leadership relies on intrinsic motivation for the performance of employees. Extrinsic motivation is any influence that is outside the individual—such as threats of punishment or promises of rewards (the old "carrot-and-stick" model). Extrinsic motivation has limited usefulness since it needs to be continually administered. Too often organizational leadership attempts to motivate people extrinsically and, unfortunately, that motivation is more often a threat.

With the fast pace at which most organizations move, it is increasingly difficult for leaders to spend time with their employees. As a result they lose touch with the human aspect of leadership. This forces them to rely on the business aspect of motivation, which is usually in the realm of extrinsic motivation. This often puts the leader in a position to seek quick fixes, such as offering monetary rewards and other incentives. The downside is that these motivators do not have sustainability. Leaders who can develop a personal relationship with their employees gain a greater sense of *why* their people work and therefore have a greater opportunity to understand the individual motivators of their people.

Intrinsic motivation is influenced from within the individual. Things like perception, self-image and individual needs all influence a person's intrinsic motivation. This motivation takes the form of a "want-to" versus a "have-to." Want-to is the phrase that we use to describe how most people approach something they enjoy doing. People don't often say they "have to" go golfing. This suggests that, in work, we don't give people the opportunity to make choices but instead tell people "what to do" and "how to do it" rather than creating the environment where they want to do it. In Love Leadership it is critically important to develop a way to understand the why's so you can create a "want-to" environment.

People are motivated by a variety of intrinsic needs. If you manage correctly, using the right intrinsic motivators, you can create unprecedented, self-sustaining energy and drive in your people. For example, a leader may be able to motivate an individual by asking for his or her opinion, involving them in a senior planning session, or giving them a challenging project and trusting them to get it done.

A 1989 management survey at a large telecommunications

company identified fourteen reasons why people worked. Interestingly, the top eight were intrinsic, and only four of the fourteen were extrinsic. Now you might be saying, hey, this data is almost twenty years old. That's true, but I bet the results would still be very close to the same.

1)	Doing work I find challenging and interesting	Intrinsic
2)	Experiencing a sense of personal achievement	Intrinsic
3)	Being treated with respect and consideration	Intrinsic
4)	Working with a management team I respect	Intrinsic
5)	Having an opportunity to develop my talents	Intrinsic
6)	Enjoying my job day in and out	Intrinsic
7)	Working with people I like	Intrinsic
8)	Having the opportunity for promotion	Intrinsic
9)	Being assured of job security	Extrinsic
10)	Having a better salary and benefits	Extrinsic
11)	Having my ideas acknowledged and put to use	Intrinsic
12)	Having greater autonomy in my job	Intrinsic
13)	Having a work location and hours that I like	Extrinsic
14)	Having better working conditions	Extrinsic

Again Margaret Wheatley can shed light on the subject. In the same interview I quoted above, she spoke of the essence of intrinsic motivation when she described a conversation she had with a woman who had recently retired as the chief of the Calgary Police Force. In an attempt to help her police force become the kind of officers they wanted to be, the chief had made it her goal to be personally available and present for each of her officers. As a leader, she was modeling the principles she stood for, and she worked with everyone to identify what they were trying to accomplish and the principles they were trying to live up to. She "worked from a very clear perspective that it's not the corporate values that count, it's whether people can enact their personal values inside the corporation. I thought that was a brilliant re-thinking of that," Wheatley said.

It's not easy, Wheatley noted: "[The chief] kept saying that this was enormously time-consuming and was very difficult work that required her to be there all the time. And so I understand why leaders don't want to go down this love path or the relationship path, because it requires so much. But that's where I think you have to want to believe in people…you really have to want to have relationships, and there are an awful lot of people in our workplaces, not just leaders but whole professions, who have never wanted relationships. They've wanted the work, and hopefully we are now realizing, most of us, how important relationships are."

How mentorship leads to good followership

Becoming a good follower is just as difficult as becoming a good leader. Good leadership, consequently, requires the ability to create good followership, but how? One way is through mentorship. Love Leadership attracts both mentors and followers. Mentors feel a responsibility to share their knowledge by coaching and fostering the progress of people around them. Followers make leadership possible. Most employees are followers-in-waiting—more than anything they want meaning in their work lives, and mentors to motivate them to find it. Thus the two go hand-in-hand. To be a good mentor you need good followers; to be a good follower, you need a strong mentor.

Mentoring is a two-way street

There are two factors I want to bring out about mentorship. The first is the importance of the mentors' having the ability to see more in people than they see in themselves, and being willing and able to find a way to draw these gifts and talents out in the person. For me this hits home on so many levels. So much of the management-driven leadership I see implies "You better do well or you'll be fired." The mentorship-driven leadership I see goes way beyond this. Great leaders have a kind of X-ray vision that can see people's hidden talents. Maybe it's actually supersonic hearing—great leaders find more inside of their people because they listen to them more carefully and thoughtfully.

The second factor is being recognized as a mentor. It's not just what you see in them that attracts people; it's what others see in you that they find inspiring. That's an interesting reflection. Think about it. If you think about it, there are individuals you see greatness in, but if they don't accept you as a mentor, you really can't do much with that greatness. You might see potential in your team, but they need to see inspiration in you. They need to trust you as a mentor and believe you can bring out that greatness. If they are inspired, they want to perform for you, win for you, help you, because you've seen things in them they can build on. Mentoring is a two-way street that creates great followership out of inspiring leadership. No successful company can afford to do without either one.

My role as a mentor

Being a successful mentor is directly linked to self-concept. The way I see myself, and the way you see me, will affect my performance. When I left SaskTel, I was given a going-away party by my group. One of my colleagues, speaking for the group, gave me a tribute in the form of a toast. "You've been a good leader, teacher and mentor to us," she said. It was a nice compliment, and I accepted it fully because I already knew that they saw me that way. They didn't want to let me down and I didn't want to let them down. It's the pebble-in-a-pond effect, where every circle created when you drop a pebble in the water expands to encompass more and more. As your capacity for Love Leadership increases, the ability to mentor increases, just as your character takes on more authenticity and vulnerability, and increases your ability to model your principles. Love, like that pebble tossed into the center of a lake, spreads out in ever-widening circles.

Let me reemphasize here that Love Leadership does not require you to go around hugging people or telling them you love them. Rather, it's something that's implied in your behavior and the way you treat others. It means there's a consciousness of the importance of love in human relationships. When someone shows they care, there's a spirit to it, a notion that we're all in this together—we're all trying to do our best. Having said that, I also think it should be a goal in organizations to create a feeling of comfort with the word "love" so that it's not a big deal to hear someone say it.

A journey, not a destination

Love Leadership is a process, an evolution, a becoming. You keep finding behaviors that fit the principles in your life and you connect them to fill out your leadership. It's a style that begins within you. A culture of love creates higher performance in an organization. It's an idealistic notion for sure, but creating greater consciousness about love, forgiveness, honesty and respect does provide a great start to bring into play many positive traits that can inform and enrich families, communities and companies.

Let's give Meg Wheatley the last word here. When asked what leaders can do to unleash love in their organizations, Wheatley replied:

> It's simple; just be loving! Why has expressing love become such a problem when it's a fundamental human characteristic? This is where I think we have over analyzed and over complexified something that is known to everyone alive. Babies know how to unleash love. It's all about our relationships and being available as a human, rather than as a role. It's about being present and being vulnerable and showing what you're feeling.

Spoken like a true Love Leader.

Chapter Eight

Overcoming Conflict the Love Leadership Way

Conflict between human beings is inevitable, whether on a personal level or in a business setting in terms of group dynamics. Everyone has opinions, feelings, beliefs and convictions that they favor in any given situation. People will often argue their position vehemently, sometimes to the point of creating a violent disagreement which, in the extreme, can paralyze an organization. Can adopting a Love Leadership style dramatically improve a high conflict situation? My unequivocal answer is a resounding yes. This does not mean that being a Love Leader means you must always agree with either one side or another no matter what just to avoid a fight. That kind of avoidance has nothing to do with love *or* leadership. So then how do you apply Love Leadership to conflicting forces within an organization or community? If you're a Love Leader and conflict emerges, do you revert to command-and-control or another default comfort level? How can you move forward in the face of conflict?

The short answer is that it takes courage. Conflict in an organization *will* make it challenging for you to maintain the integrity of your leadership style…but it can be done. I recognize that these things are easy to say; it's the doing, the acting on them, that's not quite so easy.

There is a continuum of feelings related to relationships and interacting with other people. Looking at the continuum I drew below, the further to the right you go, the more capacity you have to love. The further to the left you go, the more your capacity to love diminishes through ambivalence, disappearing into disdain and eventually, hate.

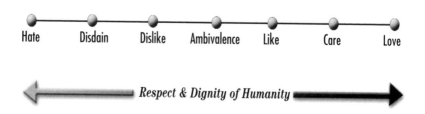

By increasing your capacity to love, you become more vigilant in protecting the dignity of others, and increase your capacity for higher performance. Conversely, if you increase your hatred, you decrease your capacity to protect the dignity of humans, and decrease your capacity for sustainable success.

I had dinner one evening in 1997 with Dr. Robert Spitzer. That night he gave me three guideposts that I have used ever since. This is what he said: "Practice love and forgiveness and be nonjudgmental." So far I have talked a lot about love and discussed the power of forgiveness that the Amish demonstrated. But how can being nonjudgmental help in conflict? Simply put, the Love Leader helps resolve conflicts by making an effort to curb his or her emotional involvement and avoid judgment. Personally, I know that I always attempt to remain curious, open, nonjudgmental and rational.

What I have found from long experience is that bringing these qualities into a situation where there is conflict is highly effective in reducing at least the degree of conflict. You might find that you still have minor disturbances or frustrations, but now your team knows that you're going to apply a Love Leadership style—and this reassures them that their personal dignity is not going to come under attack.

The first ground rule of a Love Leader is to make it clear that whatever happens, you will not in any way diminish the dignity or humanity of the individuals involved in the disagreement or dispute. As you talk about issues, if there's infringement on that ground rule, stop the discussion—that's the all-important pause between stimulus and response that everyone needs. If there is an eruption, you will need to bring to bear the other attributes of Love Leadership in order to deal with it, namely, your authenticity, principles and courage.

Love Leadership is tested by conflict

I wish I could state unequivocally that you can always, in moments of conflict, remember to approach it with a Love Leadership style. My own experience is that this is not the case. I can think of instances where my own behavior was ruled a bit less by love and more by frustration and disappointment than I would have liked. While you don't have to compromise being a Love Leader in order to deal with conflict, there are fail points in the practice of Love Leadership that will require you, like any good captain of a ship, to continually correct your course. In fact, I believe that Love Leadership is tested more in conflict than in any other situation.

In conflict, silence is not golden – courage is

Love Leadership demands that you deal head-on with issues, challenges and problems. That's where courage comes in. Not long ago I was part of a group that was trying to launch a new business. We had our share of conflicts. In one particular instance, one person in our group had done something on his own that the rest of us were not happy about. I decided that at our next meeting I would speak up about it. Frankly, I knew I should have raised the issue months earlier, but I had been reluctant to have a confrontation. It had seemed much easier to just let it slide. Besides, no one else was bringing it up—maybe it would just go away. The truth is I just didn't have the courage. But avoidance will not solve a conflict, as we all learn the hard way. Consequently, the unaddressed issue limited our ability to be open, honest and effective, and proved detrimental to what we were trying to achieve. When I finally said my piece, I expected the confrontation I had dreaded. To my surprise nobody said a word. There was no discussion, just my lonely voice, saying what I felt I had to say.

At that point, I didn't know what to think. Were the others angry with me? Had I missed something? Was I the only one bothered by this issue? As it turned out, it wasn't just me. When I pressed one of the group for a response, he told me what the others had felt: "We all thought we should have said something but none of us had the courage." Now the issue had been put out there, but was still unresolved

Although this was not a life and death issue, it absolutely impacted our overall effectiveness. I had finally mustered up the courage to speak, but it was too late for a smooth resolution. Sometimes there just is too much time lost, too much water under the bridge. This happens in many organizations. Someone's behavior is inappropriate but we don't say or do anything in a timely fashion. We adopt a "don't rock the boat" attitude. The consequence is an ineffective team and wishy-washy environment—which is not a solid foundation on which to build sustainable success.

Procedures for dealing with conflict

Conflict resolution has been studied and discussed for ages. Books have been written about it. Most institutions and companies even have written sets of procedures to deal with conflict. What I'm saying about how Love Leaders deal with conflict is well-aligned with the ideals behind those standard practices. For example, a summary of the U.S. Department of the Navy's Principles of Conflict Resolution encompasses the following suggestions and directives:

1. Think [carefully] before reacting.
2. Listen actively.
3. Assure a fair process.
4. Attack the problem, not the person.
5. Accept responsibility. [Avoid blaming others].
6. Use direct communication. [Speak from your point of view without loaded words].
7. Look for interests. [Find out what is truly at issue].
8. Focus on the future.
9. [Look for] Options for mutual gain.

This practical advice is repeated over and over, and the truth of it is obvious. It's the acting on it that's difficult—even in situations that involve professional arbitrators. I think the most challenging aspect of conflict resolution is getting to the point where you can leave your emotions out of it. Keep in mind these two actions: 1) Think before reacting. 2) Don't be the judge; be the mediator, the facilitator.

Expanding the gap between stimulus and response

In a conflict situation, it's easy to slip into patterned behaviors and get drawn in emotionally. This immediately impairs your ability to look at the situation rationally. Love Leaders have empathy. They strive to understand where another person is coming from, *their* feelings and *their* point of view. Love Leaders also make every effort to suspend judgment—to take a nonjudgmental approach to people and their opinions. This requires the ability to allow enough time between the stimulus and your response to it that you can put your love into it. Do that and you'll find yourself able to move back to being curious and interested in the larger picture, that is, what may be behind the person's behavior and motives, and in so doing gain valuable insights that can help diffuse the situation.

In another business venture, several friends and I are involved in a condominium building project on Mexico's west coast, just north of Puerto Vallarta. One of our partners has an assertive personality, which is generally admired in leaders. This man sees most issues as black or white and consequently his decisions usually are very pronounced—i.e. "This is It!" Luckily, I was in the process of editing this book on one of our trips to the building site and the principles of Love Leadership were fresh in my mind. This allowed me space between the stimulus—his arbitrary way of dealing with situations that I found frustrating—and my response. On several occasions, this partner would simply announce, "No, we're not doing it that way—we're doing it this way." He could be so abrupt that you got the sense that he hadn't heard what was said, or really thought through the options.

In business, we put great value on quick, strong-minded decision makers. But if you think about it, can a leader really be spot-on if he or she snaps out decisions that quickly? I think it creates doubt in followers. Are they announcing a decision because it sounds good or because they have given it due thought? In Mexico, I was able to not allow the emotional overtones inspired by our partner's announcements to trigger my emotions and did not become engaged in direct conflict. Because I had created a space between stimulus and response, I could be curious about everything that was happening in the moment. And, also thanks to Love Leadership, I could see the broader viewpoint. These were all my friends. I asked myself, "Do I really love this guy, even though he's so abrupt in his opinions?" Yeah, I do care for him. That realization enabled me to respond from a position of empathy rather than conflict, and allowed me to facilitate and guide us all to a mutually acceptable solution.

Conflict to resolution...not always a straight line

Conflict among team members in a boardroom or strategy session can vary widely in intensity and degree, and there *are* sometimes insurmountable obstacles. Even with a Love Leadership style, you may not resolve the conflict, but you can act with courage and authenticity. You can at least ensure that you do not harm the dignity of any individual. Even if the conflict is not resolved, it will help the process. Let's say someone is trying to take over your company. To stay true to Love Leadership when you're being threatened like that is Gandhi-level maturity, a grand ambition but an unattainable goal. Practicing your Love Leadership in certain situations may be an uphill struggle, but it is always worthwhile and will lead you farther than you can go without it.

Hate Leadership...what the world has too much of right now
Hate Leadership is of course the very antithesis of leadership based on courage, authenticity or principles, but we see it in play in corporate settings and in global conflicts. History constantly proves that responding with love, which protects the dignity and humanity of the individual, is the better path, but it certainly is not always the one we choose, as the newspaper headlines and television broadcasts tell us daily.

Dignity & Humanity

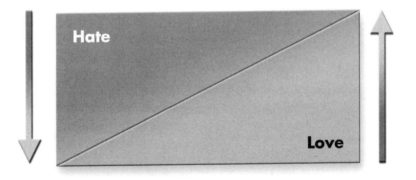

Dignity & Humanity

| **Increase** your Capacity to Hate and you **decrease** your capacity to maintain dignity and respect | **Increase** your Capacity to Love and you **increase** your capacity to maintain dignity and respect |

From mild annoyance to rage

Love Leadership may not be able to resolve every conflict, but it can diminish the intensity and degree of any and all conflicts, and it can open doors to resolution. On a scale of 1 to 5, a conflict at the lowest end (1) might be minor irritation, the center (3) might be frustration and the other extreme (5) is rage. If my conflict with a person increases to the degree of actual annoyance, I'm confident we can still work through it. But as the conflict ratchets up, so will my emotions. I then begin to move beyond annoyance to frustration, aggravation, even anger. My ability to act rationally, nonjudgmentally and with respect for the dignity of that individual is now challenged. And if it reaches a point of rage, we're at a point of crisis.

The other day I read a newspaper article about a father in my own hometown who shot and killed his daughter's drug-peddling boyfriend, who had gotten her hooked on crack. In his shoes, I might have momentarily felt moved to do the same thing, but this father has, in effect, obliterated almost everything further he could ever do or be for his daughter. When emotion escalates, your ability to view the situation rationally decreases, often dramatically.

When your emotions are engaged and your rationality inhibited, your ability to apply Love Leadership is also inhibited. It's not easy to be courageous, authentic and vulnerable when you're emotionally distraught. But I find, as I mature, that I have become more skilled at preventing myself from getting drawn in emotionally. The process starts when I allow myself more time between stimulus and response. For me, that begins with taking a few deep breaths, but there is evidence that anger can be biologically transformed.

The biological transformation of anger

In their book, *Transforming Anger: The HeartMath Solution for Letting Go of Rage, Frustration, and Irritation* (New Harbinger Publications, June 2003) Doc Childre and Deborah Rozman tell us that thoughts and feelings are stored in the nervous system and create cellular triggers of anger. Neuroscientists have discovered that getting the heart into a positive rhythm sends a signal to the brain that allows the heart and brain to communicate and together transform anger, frustration, and irritation into compassion, empathy, and calm. In order to get beyond the mechanical negative pull of their triggers, the authors maintain, you can learn to control your heart rhythms through a "freeze-frame" technique that allows you to clearly see your options for dealing with anger. While our methods may differ, that "freeze frame" is the same time and space gap I'm talking about.

If I want to live in a loving world, the standard rule is that I must resolve this conflict without harming the dignity and humanity of the person I'm having this conflict with. I have to figure out a way to solve this challenge without harming, hurting or belittling anyone. In romantic comedies the guy often can't say "I love you" to the girl because he knows if he does, it means commitment. For me, if I use the word "love" with a team, it *does* mean a commitment. It means that I'm invested in you and you're invested in me. Because I'm invested in you, I need to be able to work through any conflicts between us in a reasonable way. If I did not love you, I could just cast you off and concentrate on getting my own way. Because I *do* love you, I need to think about how I can resolve this conflict without harming the relationship.

A vital lesson my mother taught me

The person who taught me the most about dealing with conflict by using love is my mother. Fifteen years ago my sister Barrie was diagnosed with multiple sclerosis. At the time she lived in another city, where she met her husband, David. David came from a family that was quite different from ours. As his relationship with my sister evolved, we noticed that David had little use for his own family and just as little for ours. And, as Barrie's condition deteriorated, his ability to influence her to diminish her relationship with us increased. Soon, having access to our sister became a source of conflict. When I did visit, I'd tell her I loved her, and get no response. That was painful. David would interact with me to some extent, but was openly hostile to my sisters and our mother.

Then David was diagnosed with cancer, and could no longer look after Barrie. My mom went out there to help out. Imagine moving into someone's home when there's that kind of conflict waiting for you! My mom is a very loving person, and her love for her daughter overpowered her dislike of David. Pretty soon, she was looking after both of them. In all, she spent a good three or four months living with them, running errands, driving them to appointments, taking care of them in every way, including meeting their physical needs, which were considerably taxing.

Over this period, the transformation in David was amazing. He began to allow us into his home, and my sister Barrie responded to us with as much affection as she had before David came between us. Even more surprising, one day, when my children were all in the room, David said to us, "What a loving, caring human being your mom is!" Even in his suffering, he had that loving regard for my mom. Sadly, until the day he died, he still harbored disdain for his own family. That conflict was still there for him. But at least he was able to express love for us, his extended family. It was my mom's "good beyond self" behavior that brought such an unexpected, positive response out in this hurt and angry man. It was her courage, her authenticity, her willingness to be vulnerable and her ability to act with unselfish love that made the difference.

Can Love Leadership resolve conflicts, in both our professional and personal lives? Yes, you bet it can!

The Love Leadership challenge

Is this overwhelming to you? Do you feel that you would never be able to live up to this loving approach? Yes, I have presented you with a personal evolutionary challenge, one that may, at this point, feel a bit daunting. This reaction, if such is the case for you, is a positive one—it just means this is all sinking in. Please, read on....in the next chapter I am going to show you a realistic process to advance your Love Leadership style without feeling that you need to transform yourself all at once.

Chapter Nine

Evolution of a Love Leader: Progress, Not Perfection

One of the things I love about the work I do is how much I keep learning. I hope the people I coach learn half as much from me as I do from them. That is especially true for me with regard to Myrna Bentley. When I think about the evolution of a Love Leader, I often think of Myrna, who I have mentioned here before, because she is a prime example of Love Leadership in action. I learned a lot about what it takes to be a Love Leader from Myrna because that is what she is.

Myrna's career has been in the financial industry, where a certain kind of perfection was demanded of her. She had to be responsible, perform due diligence and fulfill all of the demands for transparency in a fiduciary organization. One day, she said to me, "I have to give up."

"What!" I began to protest, trying to come up with a pep talk to dissuade her from what I thought was a drastic step—her resignation.

But that was not at all what Myrna meant. She laughed and explained that it had become increasingly apparent that trying to be perfect in every situation was overly ambitious. "Progress, not perfection," she said. "That's our new motto." She recognized that while the company aspired to perfection, she needed to heavily emphasize her pleasure with every advance they made and pass lightly and forgivingly over any shortcomings along the road to progress...a laudable goal.

Progress isn't always easy to see

Another group I've worked with for several years is headed by another natural Love Leader. This woman has been highly success-ful in the company she's in. By her own admission, though, she advanced up the career ladder by transforming herself into a pre-dominantly command-and-control leader with a "masculine" style. Over the last two or three years, however, I've witnessed a trans-formation. She and her team have become authentic, compassion-ate, respectful, and prepared to be vulnerable. They are also strongly principled and think in terms of good beyond themselves. I've watched them exhibit significant characteristics of Love Leadership and develop a loving corporate culture.

Then they added a new player onto their team, also a woman.

My first observation was that this new player tended to be judgmental, which I knew could lead to conflict. I took the leader aside and advised, "I think we have to be careful how we manage this new person because I sense that there is agitation or some kind of abrasiveness between her and one or two of the other team members." Sure enough, a couple of months later, there was a con-flict. I decided to have a private meeting with the new team mem-ber, and I described my view of the team as a "love team."

"Well, that's not what I get," she said.

I found it interesting that while I was seeing a Love Leadership team, she was not. Indeed, the characteristics of Love Leadership are not always visible to everyone. She was seeing the imperfec-tions in the team and I was seeing a transformation so great that it looked like perfection. Fortunately, this woman was a respectful, competent and capable person, and eventually she integrated well into the team. As with most progress, it took time. What I learned from this experience is that classifying a person as a Love Leader can be risky because it is subjective. There are no empirical criteria to judge Love Leadership.

Is a Love Leader loving all the time?

I wish I could say that I'm consistently a Love Leader—that I'm perfect—but, of course, even as I mature and grow as a person and as a leader, there are times when I know I just don't measure up. If you are an aspiring Love Leader, you can examine yourself in two ways. One is when an event takes place and you ask yourself, "Did I demonstrate a Love Leadership style there?" The second way is more introspective, assessing your personal qualities. "Am I actually a Love Leader?" When events happen in my world, there are times I act in a loving way, and times I don't. My personal goal is to develop into a more sustainable Love Leader. I recognize that reaching those objectives is not assured—it's an evolution. It involves a transition to what is almost an idealistic level. The higher you set your sights, the further the climb to the top. Frankly, I like having almost unattainable goals. To set the bar lower is not enough for me. I don't think I'll ever reach the heights, the Mount Everest of Love Leadership, so to speak. I am not Gandhi, but I am also not satisfied with ambitions that can be easily attained and would leave me with nothing more to strive for.

Identifying Love Leaders

Once I began thinking about the attributes of Love Leadership, I started making distinctions in my own mind about how this person is a Love Leader and that one is not. As I said before, this is largely a subjective evaluation, so some of the people I would categorize as Love Leaders may not always behave that way. I might disqualify others as Love Leaders based on observing them in just two or three situations, which might not make for a fair assessment. Even Mother Teresa was human. Reportedly, she was a somewhat harsh taskmaster to the nuns in her order. In all fairness, though, she never asked more of them than she did of herself.

Take any significant public figure, call that person a Love Leader, and you run the risk of somebody disagreeing. Love Leaders, like all of us, make mistakes, get swept into old prejudices and fail from time to time to maintain their loving aims. As human beings, we take two steps forward and one back. That's okay—that's the way we are. If I had said, "I guess I'll never be a Love Leader" the first time I failed at being one, I'd have given up long ago. For me, developing this style of leadership, at work and at play, is worthy of the struggle.

Some likely Love Leaders

Now that I've explained how difficult it is to absolutely identify a Love Leader, I'd like to suggest a few people anyway. I've done a bit of reading on Warren Buffett, and from what I understand about him, he seems to me to be a Love Leader. He lives in the same relatively simple home he bought in the 1950s, and aside from that, there's story after story about his authenticity, courage and principles. He seems to be extremely solid in his convictions, especially in the arena of good beyond self versus ego gratification, as evidenced by his giving the majority of his money to The Gates Foundation. He could have set up his own philanthropic organization and gotten the ego gratification of The Warren Buffett Foundation. He chose to give it to somebody else because he believed they could distribute the money more effectively. I can't think of anyone else on the public stage who reaches his level. I've also heard that Bill Gates himself was profoundly influenced by Warren Buffet in terms of altruistic work, and it has been reported that, in fact, it was his friendship with Buffett that led to the formation of the Bill and Melinda Gates Foundation.

Jimmy Carter is another person I submit is a Love Leader. I don't have an informed opinion of Jimmy Carter as a U.S. president, but I do have a strong impression of him as a world leader post-presidency. What I see in him is authenticity, a principled viewpoint and what seems to be good beyond self. When I look at

Jimmy Carter's characteristics—and I can only judge his actions from afar—he seems to have moved into the position of one of the world's loving leaders. One objective indication is that the Nobel Prize Committee thought him worthy of the Peace Prize. I did hear Mr. Carter speak once. He was challenging the current administration, speaking with both respect and courage. You might not always expect that from a politician, but I don't get a sense that Carter is a politician anymore. I think he's genuine and authentic and very much what we think of as a statesman.

One of my favorite Canadian leaders is Stephen Lewis. To many of us, he is model of good beyond self. His courage and conviction is evident in his taking on the overwhelming challenge of the fight against AIDS in Africa. In 1984, Stephen Lewis was appointed Canadian Ambassador to the United Nations, and from 1995 to 1999, Lewis was Deputy Director of UNICEF. From 2001 until 2006, he worked as United Nations Special Envoy for HIV/AIDS in Africa. There he worked to draw attention to the AIDS crisis and alert leaders and the public to their responsibility. He has been widely praised for his effectiveness.

I also see Bill Clinton as evolving into a Love Leader. Obviously he has had some indiscretions that were offensive to some, while others wrote them off as minor character flaws. Like many people, I'm not comfortable with adultery, and to me he crossed the line. Can I forgive him? I can. Now that he's past that and into another phase of his life, he strikes me as a person with a huge and genuine capacity to love. He also continues to demonstrate an ongoing commitment to good beyond self.

The test is being effective

As I said earlier, another lesson Lou Tice taught me is that **authenticity** needs **progressiveness** and **effectiveness**. There are some people I've worked with who get to a point in their careers where they think they know it all. I don't care what they think they know, but when somebody gets to thinking that way, I'm typically concerned for them because the folks that seem to be the strongest, most effective leaders believe that there is more they don't know than what they do know. As a result, they are constantly learning. And the more they learn, the more they see that they still don't know a whole heck of a lot. So they continue to search for the knowledge and experiences that can bring them to the next level, and the next, in a never-ending quest for wisdom. That's the only way to be progressive and effective.

In terms of my Love Leadership mantra of "progress, not perfection," being as good as you can be today as an authentic Love Leader is important, but recognizing you still need to progress further is critical. I can tell you that, on a personal level, my ambition is nothing less than to increase my capacity to love in a way that encompasses the entire planet. I know I'll never reach this lofty goal, but as Robert Browning wrote, "Ah, but a man's reach should exceed his grasp, or what's a heaven for?"

When I'm working with people with whom I've worked for a long time, it is reasonably easy for me to function as a Love Leader. When I move into another organization where I don't know the people, it is far more challenging. All I'm really saying is that if you or I are going to be the best we can be, or if the human race wants to be the best it can be, we have to recognize that there is always a "next level" we need to go to in a never-ending quest to move forward. The real test is whether or not we are being effective. For me to be an effective Love Leader I have to work toward increasing my

Family ➡ Friends ➡ Company ➡ Community ➡ Country ➡ World

capacity to love others in an ever-widening circle, including my family and friends, clients, members of my community, my countrymen and people throughout the world.

At the end of the day, if I can reach that level of love the Greeks call agape, the love that cares for another motivated solely by an awareness of the intrinsic dignity of that other, then I will be getting close to where I need to be.

Love, forgiveness and being nonjudgmental

While the journey I'm on is to increase my capacity to love, I also want to increase my capacity to forgive, and not just to forgive others, but also to forgive myself. The more sensitive I become to Love Leadership, the more times I can see that "I didn't do that very well." Not long ago I made a presentation to our City Council—before the mayor and all the councillors—about building a river park. One of the city councillors is notoriously abrasive. I knew that this woman had recently been critical of a proposal to charge admission to the city's public galleries. When I made my presentation to build a water park on the river, she stood up and aggressively asked me, "Would you be charging for this?"

Knowing this individual's reputation and being slightly annoyed, I said, "Well, I live across the street from a beautiful park and the last time I checked we weren't charging admission."

She didn't say a word; she just sat back down. Later some people who don't like her wanted to high-five me because I gave her that jab, but I did not feel good about it. True, she was being disrespectful to me, but I didn't need to be disrespectful to *her.* In some situations, my buttons will be pressed, and like it or not, I'm not always going to be as authentic, progressive and effective as I'm trying to be. If I expect perfection from myself, I'm going to be disappointed. But if I expect *progress* from myself, I can achieve it.

Love Leadership is for everybody

Although we've been talking about Love Leadership largely in a business context, I hope you see that much of what I have been saying is not restricted to corporations or organizations, but applies to all aspects of life. Being authentic and courageous as a mom or dad, being authentic, courageous and vulnerable as a teacher—the same principles hold true. Running a not-for-profit or a for-profit—the style is, or should be, consistent in any situation. One is not expected to act like a Love Leader all the time. I know that, for myself, I can be immature about the smallest things. At times I'll stop and ask myself, "Why am I behaving like a two-year-old?" It is part of being human, part of having relationships, and relationships don't come in standardized shapes or sizes. If I could never worry about showing my vulnerabilities, if I could be authentic with everybody I come across, it would be quite something. All I or anyone can do is put forth our best efforts—from executives and entrepreneurs to parents, teachers, and world leaders. Progress, not perfection. Remember, the turtle won the race, not the hare.

> *"Love is the only force capable of transforming an enemy into a friend."*
> ~Martin Luther King, Jr.

Chapter Ten

Can Love Leadership Resonate Globally?

I started writing this book because I saw the need for—and the power of—Love Leadership in a corporate environment. I looked at the pitfalls of authoritarian leadership or inhumane treatment affecting morale and performance and I saw the possibility of allowing love into organizations and into leadership. I've seen Love Leadership take a company from near-bankruptcy to top performer in its field. I've seen Love Leadership work in the corporate arena, and in the personal arena. Still, the reason the subtitle of this book is "What the World Needs Now" is that my vision for this new wave of leadership, this leader-shift if you will, has expanded.

In my neck of the woods, in Canada overall, I am optimistic about the transition that I see taking place. Increasingly Canadian companies are becoming aware of the importance of improving their corporate cultures. In fact, for the last 10 to 15 years, both corporate America and corporate Canada have been trying to "flatten" their organizations into more Whiteheadian structures that bring forth co-responsibility and co-accountability. They're putting the ownership of who's responsible for the success of the organization on *everybody's* shoulders—not just on the person at the top. The very existence of the Great Place to Work® Institute and its sister organizations around the world is clear testimony that a Love Leadership-like style is steadily gaining traction.

One of Canada's success stories is WestJet Airlines, headed by Clive Beddoe, a likely Love Leader. WestJet was rated number one for having the most admired corporate culture in Canada, according to the 2006 Canadian Corporate Culture Study, published in *Canadian Business*. The company that does these yearly studies, Waterstone Human Capital Ltd., asks 185 Canadian executives, "What organizations do you most admire in terms of having a corporate culture that has helped them be successful?" Also in 2006, WestJet was rated the second-best low-cost airline in North America. Eighty-six percent of WestJet's 5,000 employees own stock in the company. WestJetters contribute an average of 13% of their base salary to the purchase of WestJet shares, and have been rewarded with $63.8 million in profit-sharing dollars over the past nine years.

A world without love

Now let's look at the dark side of the equation. What I wrote earlier about conflict as a continuum, with hate on one end and love on the other, can be applied to what is happening throughout the world. When a group or class of people, or even a nation, are engaged in an internal struggle and move on the continuum from love or like into dislike or disdain, or worse, hate of an ethnic group, country, religion or sect, it becomes easy to rationalize not protecting the dignity of those people. When people are categorized or stereotyped as enemies, it becomes easy to justify torturing and killing prisoners, or blowing up a group of innocent men, women and children in the name of a narrowly-defined "righteous" cause.

In a world where Love Leadership is the ideal, you would still have conflict, but the standard rule would be to solve each conflict without harming the dignity and humanity of another human being. There would have to be a peaceful way to solve disputes. It makes so much sense to me that I'm often astonished that the choice to lead with love isn't made more often. As Colin Powell wrote, "Discipline isn't what causes men to go into the face of enemy fire, it's counting on one another, and serving one another, and loving one another as family members." If love has the power to motivate people to lay down their lives, why can't it also have the power to motivate them to find a way to put an end to war?

Viability of Love Leadership taking hold in the world

If the natural instinct of human beings, from birth to death, is to love, in between we've created an utterly unnatural condition. It need not remain this way. My optimism comes from observing how people's capacity for love can grow as they mature. I also factor in Deepak Chopra's viewpoint. He believes that, as a species, we are evolving toward a more peaceful world. In a 2006 interview in Toronto, Chopra said that while the world is currently "divisive, quarrelsome and idiotic," it is also true that "the universe is 13.8 billion years old; human beings have only existed for 200,000 years, so we are in the infancy of our evolution and we can be a little patient with those of us who are still not in our teens. Humanity hasn't even entered its puberty yet."

Interestingly, Chopra sees his role in the world as "helping to create a critical mass of consciousness in the world that will make spirituality practical in healing the environment, in resolving conflict, in raising the economic level of poor people, and in restoring human dignity." With this aim in mind, Chopra co-founded the Alliance for a New Humanity, which links groups or communities of consciousness with each other globally so that they can spread "peace consciousness." As Chopra explains, "Peace consciousness means lots of things. It means being peace, thinking peace, feeling peace, speaking peace, acting peace, sharing peace, creating peace, celebrating peace so that every aspect of your life is devoted to peace."

If it were up to me, I'd substitute the word "love" for peace.

Love Leadership in politics

In today's environment, putting Love Leadership into politics is not an easy objective. It seems almost preordained that politicians cannot be authentic. There are undoubtedly politicians who aspire to be what I am calling a Love Leader, but, while a politician may believe there is great value in a Love Leadership style, the degree of political cynicism that's out there in the media goldfish bowl we live in makes it especially difficult for a politician to successfully maintain his or her inner Love Leader. It would be wonderful, even life-changing, to see political leaders act authentically. I am reminded of the movie "Dave," with actor Kevin Kline playing a look-alike replacement for the President of the United States. The movie ends with the "real" president courageously acting both vulnerable and authentic. This movie has great appeal because most of us really do want our world leaders to be that authentic.

Whether it's Jimmy Carter, Bill Clinton, Al Gore or Pierre Trudeau, it's interesting to see world leaders becoming more courageous and speaking more clearly and openly about what they believe after they leave office. I think perhaps that's why Martin Luther King didn't run for political office. Had he entered the political arena, he probably could not have become the advocate he wanted or needed to be. Colin Powell spoke at a global conference at a time when he was being urged to run for the presidency of the United States. As a speaker, he was very authentic. When asked if he was going to run for office, his answer was, "I don't think I could be as effective as a president as I could not being one."

However, to give a completely balanced viewpoint, while Colin Powell was U.S. Secretary of State, he had the opportunity to stand up and be authentic and honest about his negative reaction to invading Iraq, and he did not do so. In his address to the United Nations, he just "went with the program," unquestioningly providing information that later proved to be tainted. In a September, 2005 interview with Barbara Walters, Powell, who had resigned his position, was asked about that speech. He responded honestly that it was a "blot" on his reputation and that "It will always be a part of my record. It was painful. It's painful now."

A case of courage

A chapter on Harry Truman from Michael Beschloss' book *Presidential Courage*, which was excerpted in *Newsweek*, tells the story of how Harry Truman and his friend, Eddie Jacobson, through their deep friendship, helped support the creation of the State of Israel. How did that come about? If it wasn't for Eddie's gentle pressure on Truman, the president probably would not have had a pivotal meeting with Chaim Weizmann, which convinced him to support the establishment of the Jewish state. Weizmann, you may recall, became Israel's first president. There were, of course, many other factors that Truman considered at this historic point, but this chapter in Beschloss' book convinces me that Eddie Jacobson's influence on Truman was critical.

Truman was well-known for making occasional anti-Semitic remarks, but like any prejudice, it's hard to maintain when you really get to know someone on a personal level. Truman and Eddie met in 1917, and, after fighting the Germans in France, opened a men's clothing store together in Kansas City. The business failed, but the friendship lasted a lifetime. Truman's love for Eddie Jacobson led him to see the meaning and value of the State of Israel through his friend's heart and soul. The end of the chapter was very moving. Eddie was going to be Truman's guide to the new nation but died of a sudden heart attack before he could do that. When Truman went to Eddie's house to pay his respects, he broke down in tears and said, "I've lost my brother."

This story is a perfect fit for Love Leadership because it describes the limitations Truman had in not being able to love people categorized as Jews. But his conscious love for his lifelong friend opened a door to courageous world leadership that had an impact on millions of people and will resonate down the ages. This is a fundamental and absolutely critical point which demonstrates this truth: As soon as we get into a personal relationship with somebody, we can't maintain, or as easily maintain, false ideas about his or her race or religion or whatever it was that we disliked or feared when the group was an anonymous concept, and not embodied by a human being or human beings we care for.

A conflict resolved peacefully

In Quebec, for several decades, there has been a political party that advocates separatism. Because our political system doesn't discriminate against people who advocate secession from the country, several separatists have even been elected to our federal government. In 1995 or 1996 this issue came to a head with a referendum in Quebec for the people to vote on the issue of separation. Fortunately for folks who love Canada as it is, as I do, the majority didn't vote in favor of separating. But there was a vote, and, had it passed, Quebec would be a separate country. I was listening to a call-in talk show around that time. An American called in and said, "I don't know any place on the planet that would have handled that situation like you did in Canada." It's true—it was handled well, with respect for the dignity and humanity of people with a different point of view.

In Canada, we went through a mature, systematic democratic process that said, "Here's what you can do if you disagree." Because of that, what could have been high conflict, wasn't. I'm not saying the process was facilitated by Love Leadership, but I am saying that it was along those lines, and a mature way to deal with conflict. If conflict can be resolved peacefully, why should the human race think that war—killing people until one faction or another gives up—is the only way to solve a problem? And let's look even more deeply at this. With most wars there is often not even a clear winner or loser—just a lot of wonderful young   people who have given their lives, their limbs, or their sanity, for a fight that nobody really understands in the first place, and which ends, as the T.S. Eliot poem goes, "Not with a bang but a whimper."

What the world needs now

Can Love Leadership resonate globally? My opinion is that it must. The current way isn't working for us. In the long run, if you give hate, that's what you get back. If you give love, you may not get it back immediately, but continue to give it, and eventually you are going to get love back. It's an idealistic viewpoint, but everything of significance in our world that has been achieved was originally seen as an impossible dream. Believe in love enough to act with it and from it, and you can help transform the world we all share.

In his book, *Man's Search for Meaning*, Victor Frankl, the Holocaust survivor and psychoanalyst wrote: "A thought transfixed me: for the first time in my life I saw the truth as it is set into song by so many poets, proclaimed as the final wisdom by so many thinkers. The truth—that love is the ultimate and the highest goal to which man can aspire. Then I grasped the meaning of the greatest secret that human poetry and human thought and belief have to impart: *The salvation of man is through love and in love.*"

Afterword

Leaving a Legacy

Leaving a legacy is, to me, more than just what we leave behind after we depart from this earth. I use the term to also mean how we are remembered, as we move from one company, organization or project to another. Yes, the ego is always involved, but a bit of vanity can be a good thing. Our individual identities, our egos, are all part of what motivates us to do well, and to leave other people at least somewhat better off for having known us.

As a Love Leader, your legacy, how you are remembered, is determined not so much by what you do, but how you do it. To me, the "how" has a more pervasive influence and depth than the "what." How you do things—ideally with principled, authentic, courageous, loving leadership—includes the mentorship role you assume, and the strength of the followership you engender.

Part of my own vanity is that I want to look good. This drives me to run, to work out regularly and to eat well. My ego about wanting to leave a mark, to share what I have learned, to "pass on" my lessons learned, and, in particular, my conclusions about the urgent need for Love Leadership to help improve businesses, personal interactions, and the quality of life on this planet are what compelled me to write this book.

Never satisfied with "good enough"

One of my early mentors was the CEO of a major research organization. I got to know him in the last year or so before his retirement, when I was just beginning my career as an independent consultant. The love Jim had for his executive team and staff was obvious to me, as was the fact that it was reciprocated—not that any of them would have called it love in those days. One day, as I arrived for an appointment with Jim, I learned that it was his last day on the job. That he was taking the time to see me was a surprise. I hadn't known him long and I wasn't his best buddy or an old colleague. Nevertheless, he gave me his complete attention. Jim's legacy was that he left the organization in better shape than when he got there; but he told me he wished he had done more. That is the sentiment of a true leader; even on your last day, you wish you could have done more.

Leave more than you take

Most leaders, as they work to meet this year's goals, also stay on course for a business plan or strategy that may stretch five years into the future. Looking ahead, a mature leader thinks about what he or she is going to leave behind for the next leader or leaders. Legacy is about leaving something behind that has value to the people on your team or in your sphere of influence.

For me, this whole book, the whole notion of Love Leadership, is about leaving more in the world than I take out. That's the driving force behind legacy. It comes from a sense of accountability and responsibility—the good beyond self you've managed to achieve. How do you provide guidance beyond your own presence? Love Leadership is a style by which you encourage and nurture people rather than just "manage" them, so that they'll embody and model the attributes you've modeled for them and carry on the legacy you've begun. This also allows your legacy to reach beyond the organization, as the people you touch carry these attributes forward into their lives and their communities.

Types of leadership strengths

As you examine leaders more closely, whether from the vantage point of business, politics, science or society, you discover that there are certain individuals who seem to go beyond the everyday, inspiring people around them to reach higher. They are somehow able to draw people together to work for a common cause. These leaders are not only visible on national and international stages, but in local communities. By effectively mentoring a new generation of upcoming leaders, these leaders have created a legacy that will impact the future. They have fostered engagement and involvement through willing followership.

A few years ago, my friend Randy asked if I would offer him leadership coaching, which has become a growing part of my consulting work. Randy had excellent management skills and the natural instincts of a Love Leader. He's authentic, willing to be vulnerable, principled, courageous, and, while he definitely cares about success, he also cares about people. When he called and asked for coaching, I was curious to learn what the issues were. "Maybe I'm just a manager," he said. For me, that clarified the issue. Randy didn't feel like a leader. He had been a successful manager for most of his career, but now that he had been moved into a more responsible position he expected more of himself. Though he intuitively understood that there was more to being a leader than good management, he wasn't sure what was required.

To me, good leaders must do four basic things.

1) Provide clarity of direction so that everyone can see what you can see;

2) Develop clear measurements of success or progress;

3) Clearly define a compelling "why"; and

4) Hold people accountable to those measures, themselves included.

When any one of these elements is missing, the result within the organization or team is confusion, frustration and diminished performance.

I also believe there are four distinct roles of leadership.

Some leaders are good managers; they get the job done. Some leaders are good strategists; they know how to navigate complex markets and provide their organizations with a strategic advantage. Here Lee Iacocca comes to mind. Some leaders are visionaries, people who reimagine a business and even the world in new ways, like Henry Ford and Steve Jobs, to name just two. Lastly, there are leaders who are good in a crisis, such as Sir Winston Churchill. These characteristics are not exclusive. While most leaders have a natural tendency toward one particular leadership strength, there is usually an ebb and flow, a combination of strengths in an ongoing process.

I should also point out that there is another category of leadership, one I call the "Event Leader." A perfect example is the late Canadian athlete Terry Fox. When cancer struck him, Terry struck back. He became famous for the Marathon of Hope, a cross-Canada run to raise money for cancer research, running with one prosthetic leg. He is considered one of Canada's greatest heroes of the 20th Century and is celebrated internationally every September as people participate in the Terry Fox Run, the world's largest one-day fundraiser for cancer research. His legacy of courage lives on to this day.

It is not necessary, as a Love Leader, to sacrifice any of these leadership qualities. On whichever level he or she operates, the Love Leader is one who first and foremost invests in people. You can be a good manager/leader and a Love Leader; a good visionary and a Love Leader; good in a crisis and a Love Leader. Leadership styles that clash with Love Leadership are those in which a scarcity or superiority mentality predominate.

The legacy you leave your children

My wife and I have three kids, and we consciously and continuously explore and examine our parenting skills. We asked ourselves which was more important—having a child who is highly accomplished at certain things, or having a child who models the principles we stand for? We enjoy and encourage our children's talents and achievements, but for us there is no greater compliment than for our kids to have an enduring commitment to love. That's the legacy we want to have them carry forward.

A culture or a consciousness?

Consciousness is embedded. It takes root and grows in the heart, mind and soul. Culture is less permanent; it is a reaction to environment. When circumstances change, culture often follows, and can change drastically. Consciousness stays. Looked at this way, the legacy of Love Leadership is the consciousness you create in an organization, a family, the world.

Take this further into "being." I believe every organization has a "being" to it, a soul that carries beyond one individual leader. Embedding a Love Leadership style in the consciousness of your organization means that the legacy you leave will be holistic and sustainable.

The question of legacy

Actions and inactions have impact. If your actions are ethical, honorable and effective, they leave a positive mark; if not, they leave a negative mark. One leader I have observed over the past decade has made many positive contributions to his organization. Yet, in the last part of his career, he moved into an opinionated, antagonistic stance. I worry about his legacy. What I see is that all the good things he's done in the past may well be swallowed up by his present hostile attitude, which is all people may remember him for.

I've seen leaders, as they near retirement, lose momentum or direction, and start coasting—just riding things out. With that attitude, they tend to resist change and don't want to take on any major new initiatives. The clock is ticking, and not just for them but for their organization. I've also seen leaders who pick up the pace as they near retirement. They're on a mission to leave a mark, to make the business bigger, better, stronger than it was before. They're open to change, to new directions, to major initiatives. Their whole focus is to ensure the groundwork is laid for future growth. That's a legacy.

The human desire to be loved

After 20 years of consulting experience, I firmly believe leaders want their people to respect and trust them. I am not sure they would publicly admit that they want to be loved, but I bet you deep down in their hearts they do. If you're a consultant brought in to do a job and then move on, you may not care whether people like you or not. But if you've invested the bulk of your career in a company, you probably would care. Even then, your focus would probably be on the people you worked closest with rather than on the whole company "loving" you. It goes back to Warren Buffet's words: "For me, if the people who you hope love you, do, that's success."

What legacy will *you* leave? How would you like to be remembered? Is what you created—in your workplace, in your home and in the world at large—sustainable, so that others can pick up the torch and run with it? Did you love people enough? If not, you still have time.

For me, legacy comes down to how you want to be remembered and what you want to leave behind. I'd like to leave a legacy as a good manager, strategist, visionary, and good in a crisis. But given a choice of one, my bias is that I'd rather have made a difference with people than with things. I would love to be remembered for what I did, but if I had to choose between what I did and how I did it I would rather be remembered for how I did it—with principled, authentic, courageous, loving leadership.

Love Leadership, as I've said throughout the book, is good for business, good for your personal life…heck, it will probably even keep you alive a lot longer. By now, I hope you're with me on this. We need as many people as possible to help turn this ship around, so that we can, together, sail into smoother waters. To be part of this evolution—or, perhaps, even, *revolution*—means authentically and courageously committing to act from a place of good beyond self and to be willing to promote and preserve human dignity in any and all situations.

In closing, let me be so bold as to challenge you to unleash the natural love inside you. The promise, in evolving your Love Leadership, is that in so doing, you will without question, and without even noticing it as it happens, slowly but surely become profoundly more effective and satisfied in all areas of your life.

Gregg Cochlan

A Conversation with Gregg*

1. What is *Love Leadership* about – both the book and the concept behind it?

First, I think it's important to say what it is not. The idea of a new Love Leadership style radiating out into the world, beginning with business, is not a return to New Age, 60's kumbaya moments where we end by all hugging each other. Not that hugging is bad, mind you. I am all for it, as appropriate. But what I am writing about centers on interpersonal relationships, specifically an evolution from the personality-driven, "win friends and influence people" style of leadership, and the autocratic, top-down, domineering "do as I say" style of leadership, and even the rigid, intellectual "here are the 6, 7 or 10 rules" style, to a way of leading that always makes sure people are valued for their humanity under all circumstances. I mean, even when they have to be chastised, or fired, they are always left with their dignity. Love Leadership is about driving the fear out of your organization so that people can perform at their highest level. It is about you as a leader being authentic, vulnerable, courageous and principled, with the intent to do good beyond yourself. It is about getting better results in your life and helping others to do the same, whether personally, professionally or organizationally. This may sound simple, and it is, of course, always easier said than done, but I am absolutely convinced that this style of leadership is exactly what we need now in all areas of life.

2. Why did you write *Love Leadership*, and why did you write it now?

Even a few years back, the world may not have been ready for this type of book, for this message of bringing a love-based style of leadership into the corner offices, conference and board rooms – and into other areas of human endeavor, such as politics, government, learning institutions, the medical profession, law enforcement, nonprofit organizations, athletics and more. However, times *have* changed. While people once winced at an executive openly saying he "loved" a colleague or employee, now it's much more accepted. The discomfort level is far lower than a decade ago, when I said I loved a team member in a meeting and people rolled their eyes and couldn't even look at me. Now coaches openly express their love for their athletes. World leaders speak of love. Well, not enough of them do, but the tide is turning. I simply wanted to put a name to a new style of leadership that I was seeing, so that others could see it as well, with the ultimate hope of making it normal versus what may currently be seen as abnormal. I want to ride that wave, keep that momentum going. Whatever I can do will be a contribution. I actually felt it was my responsibility and obligation to share this with others – kind of paying-it-forward to other leaders, perhaps leaving a legacy. I talk about the idea of legacy in the book...how we each need to examine the legacy we will leave, and if we think we can do better, make the necessary changes now, putting into the action the meaning of those famous words: "If it is to be, it is up to me."

3. How did you gain your insights into Love Leadership?

It was a process, mostly experiential, but supported by my purposeful study of leadership and also, through my experience with my family, my parents, my sisters, my aunts, uncles, friends and colleagues. Plus being part of The Pacific Institute, led by the extraordinary Lou Tice, definitely helped. The greatest insights came through my consulting and working with hundreds, if not thousands of leaders, where I saw what worked and what didn't. Another eye-opener was working as a consultant with some wonderful people who are what I consider natural Love Leaders, for example, Myrna Bentley, who is described in the book. It always bothered me, when I worked in some seriously "buttoned down" corporate environments, that you couldn't express your feelings without some negative judgment settling over you like a dark cloud and poisoning the atmosphere. I also saw firsthand how Love Leadership positively impacted companies, teamwork, levels of employee job satisfaction, and ultimately the degree of success a company could hope to achieve. So again, it was a slow but steady process that brought me to understand the need for this new kind of leadership. At the least I wanted to label it, in order to make it more easily understood. Overall, I wrote this book to help people increase their capacity to love and allow love into their style of leadership.

4. What does it mean to redefine and reinvent one's self as a Love Leader?

I think it begins with taking a good hard look at yourself and what you stand for. Do you stand for integrity, honesty and courage? Do you encourage open and honest communication and even welcome intelligent "push back" when people don't agree with you? If you demand respect, do you also give respect? Some people pay lip service to having this kind of a culture, but when it comes down to it, they want people to follow them blindly. In the book I talk about the differences between values and principles. With Love Leadership, principles win out every time. A group of criminals may have a value system they all adhere to where you can kill people and it's just "business" but you don't ever kill the women and children. That may be a value, but it's hardly a principle. As Stephen Covey says, principles are "true north" – your moral compass. There are universal principles. There is absolute right and wrong, and a Love Leader's behavior is guided by these. I use an example in the book about how one company was in desperate circumstances financially and had to fire hundreds of employees, many of whom had been with them for years. The way they did it was ugly and demeaning. There were much better ways to do it that still would have resulted in layoffs, but would have allowed people their dignity rather than openly humiliating them, as was done. The more authentic and principled you are, the easier it becomes to do the right thing, to make the right decisions, because these come from who you really are deep down as a human being. Individuals who know who they really are – well, there's no pretense in them. They're effective leaders because they behave in a loving way, and that way has people respond back to them in a loving way. It's amazing to see. By the way, on a family level, if you see siblings who connect with each other, very often it's because they had a loving leader – their parents were good role models. As a rule, the best teamwork and performance comes from people who know they are loved and appreciated.

5. How would you classify this book – as a business book or as something else?

I began writing this book for business and clearly this is a book that speaks to business owners, business executives, and managers, people "in charge." But as I got further into writing the book, it became increasingly difficult to delineate when the Love Leadership relationship to business ended and its relationship to family or life began. I am hoping that all people find this book valuable because love and leadership are not confined to one area or the other. It is not written as a business book per se, which is why the subtitle is "What the World Needs Now." Two favorite books of mine are by Canadian author Robin Sharma, who wrote *The Monk Who Sold His Ferrari* and by Spencer Johnson, who wrote *Who Moved My Cheese*. Both books are wonderfully written for everyone to read, whether or not they are in business, because they speak to human nature. I would hope that *Love Leadership* is like that, that it can speak to and inspire anyone, whether they lead a business, a family, a team, an institution or a nation.

6. What barriers exist to Love Leadership as a dominant style?

Unfortunately, many people still believe that you can't motivate people by being authentic and showing vulnerability, that you need to use a command-and-control style. To me, these are leaders who are afraid to seem weak in any way. Being authentic and vulnerable are actually not weaknesses. They are strengths. I go into this at length in the book. We have a fear-based and, of course, in many ways still homophobic culture where men are afraid to express love for another man. Telling another man that you love him, as a way of expressing how deeply you appreciate and value him, does not mean you love him romantically. But we have to face the obstacles. And for women too, trying to be "macho" doesn't work – that's another authenticity issue that I talk about. Thankfully, these concepts, these holdovers from an earlier, more repressive age, are losing power. Men are now hugging their sons. The younger kids today are more open and expressive about loving each other.

7. Is it realistic to believe that Love Leadership is an evolutionary possibility?

I am an idealist and an optimist, so the answer is, yes, I do think it's realistic. I also think it makes common sense. When we're born, we're all about love. In our later years, most of us, facing death, "soften" and become more about love. What happens to us in between? "Ay, there's the rub," as Shakespeare's Hamlet says. That's when we're raising our families, making our fortunes, competing – often from a scarcity rather than an abundance point of view. So what we do is put "love" on the back burner for a few decades, except for romantic or sexuality-based love, the love of our children, or a kind of vague, generalized "love of humanity." Deepak Chopra believes, and I agree, that the collective consciousness on the planet is changing, that it is gradually becoming more peaceful. It may be difficult to find evidence of this if we go to the news broadcasts, but like Deepak, I am optimistic that there is a positive sea change underway. I am hopeful that there will be many more Love Leaders in the years ahead, and that they, in what Malcolm Gladwell would characterize as a "tipping point," will change the world to a more mature, loving place.

8. What do you hope your readers will be left with when they read this book?

I would like each reader to be left with a sense of urgency about transforming his or her own style of leadership, and a conviction and confidence that, in so doing, he or she can become a Love Leader and impact every person they interact with. I'd also like them to be open to leaving a positive legacy that can make this planet a better place. If Love Leadership does become the new paradigm, it will only be because individuals are willing to change. The more capacity to love you have, the more you exhibit and manifest it, the less defensive and judgmental we become. I keep returning to that quote by Warren Buffet, the second richest man on the planet, who said that his measurement of success is that the people you hope love you, do. I strive to get to a point where each day I am increasing my capacity to love, and I hope this book inspires readers to consider doing the same.

I end Chapter 10 with a quote from Victor Frankl, the Holocaust survivor and esteemed psychoanalyst and author. He wrote how just thinking about love was what saved him and another prisoner in one of the concentration camps. His conclusion was: "The salvation of man is through love and in love."

I dream of having a peaceful, loving resolution to conflict, which can be the new normal. That, simply stated, is what this book is all about – making the commitment on a personal and planetary level to take it up a notch. I want my readers to be genuine, fearless, courageous and adventurous. I want them to do any and everything that increases their capacity to love. I want them to mentor others. There is way too much anger, hurt, revenge, passivity and hopelessness in the world today. I think Love Leadership is a big part of the answer. I hope that people will read this book, and that it will help them see that there is a far better way to be than giving in and giving up.

*from www.loveleadership.com

Suggested Reading

Tice, Louis E. *Personal Coaching for Results: How to Mentor and Inspire Others to Amazing Growth.* Nashville, TN: Thomas Nelson Publishers, 1997.
I owe Lou my biggest debt. It was he who helped create a spirited desire in me to reach higher, do more, and strive to be progressive and effective. This book, in particular, challenged me to ask myself what and who am I waiting for? Most important was his sage advice that I need to live my life on purpose, not by accident. You will see evidence of Lou's guidance throughout my book.

Frankl, Victor E. *Man's Search for Meaning.* Beacon Press, 1959.
Also a must-read. There are more lasting life lessons in this book than I could possibly list.

Buckman, Robert. *Can We Be Good Without God? Behavior, Belonging and the Need to Believe.* Prometheus Books, 2002.
Of all the books I am suggesting, this one is the most controversial, but I encourage everyone to read it. Allow me to warn you that it may change some of your most fundamental beliefs. Like most of the books on this list, it challenged me to ask myself why we each do what we do.

Spitzer, Robert J. *The Spirit of Leadership: Optimizing Creativity and Change in Organizations.* Executive Excellence Publishing, 2001.
Dr. Spitzer's book, although somewhat academic, offers remarkable insights into spirited leadership, and provides great clarity of purpose about living an ethical life. I am personally deeply indebted to Dr. Spitzer for this simple gift of advice which he gave me one night over dinner He said, "Consider living your life with these three words: love, forgiveness and nonjudgmental."

Levoy, Gregg Michael. *Callings: Finding and Following an Authentic Life*. Harmony Books, 1997.

This is a book that contains many little gifts. One that particularly influenced me is a game Levoy played with his father when he was a boy. It's called the "Alien Game," because you pretend to be a human guide to visiting aliens, or vice versa. It's an enjoyable way to look at things without the layers of judgment and attitudes we tend to acquire, returning to the childlike sense of wonder and curiosity we often lose as adults. Levoy asks a great question: "What would you preach about if you were given an hour of prime time?" Today, the answer for me would be the topic of this book.

Chopra, Deepak. *The Seven Spiritual Laws of Success: A Practical Guide to the Fulfillment of Your Dreams*. Amber-Allen Publishing, 1994.

I enjoy all of Deepak's books, and this book especially, thanks to the lifelong lessons it offers, which I am continually trying to put into practice.

Coonradt, Charles A. *The Game of Work: How to Enjoy Work as Much as Play*. Deseret Book Company, Random House Trade Publications, 1999.

It has been 20 years since I was introduced to Coonradt's book, but every once in a while I am reminded of his ideas about making work a game. It puts things on a "want-to" rather than a "have- to" level and is a wonderful little read.

Covey, Stephen R. *The Seven Habits of Highly Effective People*. New York: Simon & Schuster Inc., 1989.

When Covey first published this book, many of my colleagues and clients rushed toward it. Its most profound lesson for me was how to move from personality to character-driven leadership. Covey clearly rang the warning bell for all of us about the need to get grounded in things that really matter, and know what we stand for.

Hamel, Gary and C.K. Prahalad. *Competing for the Future.* Harvard Business School Press, 1994.
One of the key takeaways for me in this insightful book was the notion of corporate genetic cloning, a concept that rang true for me. I saw it in my own corporation and in many of the companies I worked with. The authors are correct in describing how this phenomenon limits our ability to see other possibilities.

His Holiness the Dalai Lama. *An Open Heart: Practicing Compassion in Everyday Life.* Little, Brown and Company, 2001.
I enjoy everything I read by the Dalai Lama. This book in particular offers something I aspire to achieve: opening your heart to compassion every day.

I also recommend the following books:

Ban Breathnach, Sarah. *Simple Abundance: A Daybook of Comfort and Joy.* New York: Warner Books, Inc, 1995.

Bennis, Warren and Burt Nanus. *Leaders: The Strategies for Taking Charge.* New York: Harper and Row, 1985.

Boyett, Joseph H. and Jimmie T. *The Guru Guide: The Best Ideas of the Top Management Thinkers.* New York: Wiley, 2nd Revised Edition, 2000.

Byham, William C. *Zapp! The Lightning of Empowerment: How to Improve Productivity, Quality, and Employee Satisfaction.* Development Dimensions International, 1989.

Cameron, Julia. *The Artist's Way: A Spiritual Path to Higher Creativity.* New York: Putnam Books, 1992.

Clemmer, Jim. *Pathways to Performance: A Guide to Transforming Yourself, Your Team, and Your Organization.* Toronto: Macmillan, 1995.

Covey, Stephen R. *Principle-Centered Leadership*. Simon & Schuster New York: Summit Books, 1991.

Day, Laura. *Practical Intuition: How to Harness the Power of Your Instinct and Make It Work for You*. New York: Villard, 1996.

Foot, David. *Boom, Bust Echo: How to Profit From the Coming Demographic Shift*. Toronto: MacFarlane Walter & Ross, 1996.

Goleman, Daniel. *Emotional Intelligence: Why It Can Matter More than IQ*. Toronto: Bantam, 1995.

Hagen, Steve. *Buddhism Plain and Simple*. Charles E.Tuttle Company, 1997.

Hill, Napoleon. *Think and Grow Rich!* New York: Fawcett Crest, 1963.

Jamison, Kaleel. *The Nibble Theory and the Kernel of Power*. New York: Paulist Press, 1984.

Kohn, Alfie. *Punished by Rewards: The Trouble with Gold Stars Incentive Plans, A's, Praise, and other Bribes*. Replica Books, 2001.

Kotter, John P. *Corporate Culture and Performance*. Free Press, 1992.

Mandino, Og. *The Return of the Ragpicker*. New York: Bantam Books, 1992.

_____. *Mission Success!* New York: Bantam Books, 1986.

_____. *The Spellbinder's Gift*. New York: Bantam Books, 1995.

_____. *Twelfth Angel*. New York: Bantam Books, 1993.

_____. *The Greatest Miracle in the World!* New York: Bantam Books, 1986.

McNally David. *Even Eagles need a Push, Learning to Soar in A Changing World*. New York, Dell Reprint Edition, 1994.

Peck, M. Scott. *The Road Less Traveled: A New Psychology of Love, Traditional Values, and Spiritual Growth*. New York: Simon and Schuster, 1978.

Pilzer, Paul Zane. *God Wants You to Be Rich*. Simon & Schuster, 1995.

Powell, Colin and Joseph E. Persico. *My American Journey.* New York: Ballantine Books, 1995.

Redfield, James. *The Celestine Prophesy: An Adventure.* New York: Warner Books, 1993.

_____. *The Tenth Insight: Holding the Vision.* New York: Warner Books, 1996.

Seligman, Martin E. *Learned Optimism: How to Change Your Mind and Your Life.* New York: Knopf, 1991.

_____. *The Optimistic Child.* New York: Knopf, 1993.

Sharma, Robin. *The Monk Who Sold His Ferrari: A Fable About Fulfilling Your Dreams & Reaching Your Destiny.* Harper Collins Publishers, 1999.

_____. *The Greatness Guide: Powerful Secrets for Getting to World Class.* Harper Collins Publishers, 2006.

Smith, Hyrum W. *The 10 Natural Laws of Successful Time and Life Management: Proven Strategies for Increased Productivity and Inner Peace.* Warner Books, 1994.

Terrell, Glenn, Ph.D. *The Ministry of Leadership: Heart and Theory.* Pacific Institute Publishing, 2002.

Tice, Louis E. *Smart Talk for Achieving Your Potential.* Nashville, TN: Thomas Nelson Publishers, 1995.

About the Author

Gregg Cochlan is a leadership coach, strategic change architect, and performance management consultant. As founder and president of thinc., Corporate Change Architect and proud affiliate of The Pacific Institute, Gregg has helped industry leaders deal with the challenges of change since 1986. His experience and cutting-edge thinking enables leaders to evaluate their organizations and successfully effect change. Gregg's extensive coaching and strategic planning experience with corporations in private and public sectors includes clients in such diverse arenas as grain handling, government, the pharmaceutical industry, telecommunication, and not-for-profit organizations. Over the years, many of his clients have evolved into Love Leaders, and report profoundly higher rates of employee involvement, accountability and goal achievement, along with extraordinary improvements to their bottom line.

A native Canadian, Gregg and his wife of 28 years, Sandra, live in Saskatoon, Saskatchewan with their three children, Katelyn, Avery and Brogen.

Read more at www.loveleadership.com